Preservation and the Management of Library Collections

Second Edition

Preservation and the Management of Library Collections

Second Edition

John Feather

Professor of Library and Information Studies,
Pro-Vice-Chancellor, Loughborough University

Library Association Publishing
London

Published by
Library Association Publishing Ltd
7 Ridgmount Street
London WC1E 7AE

First published 1991
Second Edition 1996

British Library Cataloguing in Publication Data
A catalogue record for this book is available from The British Library

ISBN 1-85604-190-5

Typeset from author's disk in 10/13 pt Baskerville and Poppl-Laudatio by Library Association Publishing.
Printed and made in Great Britain by Bookcraft (Bath) Ltd, Midsomer Norton, Avon.

CONTENTS

Preface   vii
Acknowledgments   ix
1   **Preservation: a problem defined**   1
    A brief history   3
    New directions   7
    Preservation in Britain   11
       Further reading   16

2   **Media, materials and the environment**   17
    The materials of information storage   17
    Book materials   17
    Book structures   26
    Non-book materials   29
    Non-printed materials   30
    Environments for storage and use   34
    Summary   47
       Further reading   50

3   **The preservation of information**   51
    Introduction   51
    The origins and storage of digital information   54
    The selection of digital information for preservation   57
    Storage and access   67
    Digitization as a preservation tool   72
    Conclusions   75
       Further reading   76
       A note on terminology   76

4 **Preservation policy and library use** 78
Introduction 78
The demands of clients 79
The quality of the stock 82
The use of information 84
Making the choices 91
Conclusions 95
Further reading 96

5 **The physical dimension of preservation** 97
Introduction 97
The preservation survey: buildings 98
The preservation survey: collections 100
The purpose of the survey 103
Using the surveys 104
Conclusion 123
Further reading 124

6 **Preserving information: policy development and implementation** 125
Introduction 125
Preservation policy: the elements 125
Preservation administration 126
Training for preservation 137
Conclusion 139
Appendix Guidelines on preservation policies 139

7 **The professional context: preservation and access** 141
Introduction 141
The British experience 144
European experiences: France, Germany and elsewhere 147
Beyond Europe: the USA and Australia 151
The world stage: IFLA and UNESCO 153
Conclusion – but not the end 155
The future 157

References 159
Index 177

PREFACE

The first edition of this book was published in 1991 as a guide to the new approach to preservation management which had evolved during the 1980s. No longer the esoteric preserve of the rare book librarian or the archivist, preservation was seen as one of the tools of collection management to ensure access to books and information by library users. In this second edition, the fundamental concept remains unchanged: unless we preserve information, we cannot give access to it, and I repeat here the last three paragraphs of the original Preface:

> The preservation of information in an accessible form is the subject of this book. It is not a book about bookbinding or paper repair. It is a book about professional librarianship and library management, and it is intended for those whose professional concern is (or will be) with the effective management of the information resource which lies at the heart of every information agency. Whether that resource is a stock of books, or a collection of historical documents, or the discs and tapes of a database is irrelevant. Without access to information in a retrievable form, an information agency has no purpose, and so ultimately, somewhere, that information must be held in a format which has a physical existence. The survival of the information is therefore dependent upon the survival of the medium in which it is held. The preservation of information is therefore a central professional issue, and it is thus that it is presented here.

> At the core of this book is a consideration of how a preservation policy is developed and managed, but technical matters cannot be ignored. If all our information-carrying media were permanent and incorruptible,

there would be no preservation problem. But they are not, and they never can be. All of them are physical objects with a chemical constitution. None of them is entirely inert or stable. An understanding of the basic scientific facts of information storage systems is essential to an understanding of how to preserve the information itself. Such matters as the chemistry of paper or the reaction of photographic film to sunlight need not concern us in detail, but those who seek to preserve information held in those formats need to know enough about them to ensure that they are stored and used in a way which is indeed consistent with their continued existence.

There is no necessary conflict between preservation and access. Our professional business is to transfer information from where it is held to where it is needed. That is facilitated, not inhibited, by the proper storage of the information itself. Therein lies the theme and the message of this book.

There have, however, been some very real changes in the six years since the book was written, and this edition edition intends to take account of them. The revision has been thorough and comprehensive: a new chapter on electronic information has been added, and the topic will also be addressed in other chapters; the section dealing with technical issues, and especially with scientific developments such as mass deacidification and digitization, has also been enlarged; throughout, I have tried to take account of recent research and the current literature.

A wholly new feature of this edition are the notes on further reading at the end of each of the first five chapters. These point the way to more detailed reading on the subject of the chapter, and augment the references at the end of the book.

I hope that, in this rewritten form, this book will continue to be as useful as I have been told the first edition was. It is intended to be of service to the practitioner as well as the student; in particular, librarians and other information workers who are beginning to come to terms with the issues raised by the need to preserve both information and information carriers should find something here to guide and to help them.

ACKNOWLEDGMENTS

My first thanks go to Helen Carley of Library Association Publishing, who suggested that the time had come for a revised edition of this book and supported me throughout the writing of it.

Once again, I thank my students in the Department of Information and Library Studies at Loughborough University. Those who have taken the courses on the preservation of library materials will recognize some of the material and ideas in this book. The classes of 1994–5 and 1995–6, in particular, were the first recipients of some of the new parts of this edition. I am grateful to them for their tolerance and for that of my colleagues Graham Matthews and Paul Eden, who contributed more than they may realize. My colleague Alan Poulter helped with the Note on Terminology in Chapter 3 and provided many valuable comments on the whole of that chapter.

More broadly, I have been fortunate enough to discuss preservation with many of those most involved in it, in both the United Kingdom and overseas. None of them can be held responsible for what is here, and some may even disagree with a few of my ideas. Nevertheless, Jean-Marie Arnoult, Terry Belanger, David Clements, Josephine Fang, Graham Matthews, Fred Ratcliffe, Merrily Smith and Michael Turner all, in their various ways, influenced the first edition. To their names I must now add others: Mirjam Foot the Director of Collections and Preservation at the British Library, London, for – among many other things – access to a late stage of the draft of the ISO document on storage of library and archival material, Helen Forde, Ross Harvey and John McIntyre. My secretary, Cynthia Robinson, continues to cope with

has played a key role in the completion of this book. Finally, I would like to thank the reviewers of the first edition for their generosity and especially Ellen Macready, whose criticisms were as helpful as her sociology was perverse.

John Feather
Pro-Vice-Chancellor
Loughborough University

Chapter 1
PRESERVATION: A PROBLEM DEFINED

The central task of the librarian is to make information available to users. To achieve this it is necessary to organize, both physically and intellectually, the media that contain information. This, however, is a futile operation if either the documents themselves or the information they contain, are not available for consultation. The information, the *raison d'être* of the document, will indeed be lost if the medium that carries it is not preserved in a usable form. This apparent truism has been somewhat eclipsed in recent years, but an understanding of its implications is fundamental to the effective provision of information to users.

The development of new media of information storage to supplement the traditional written or printed documents has been a significant element in the growth of this neglect. The new information media are, for the most part, comparatively easy to replicate, so their physical preservation seems of little importance. Much of the information for which such media are used is, in any case, considered by its originators to be of comparatively short-term interest, since it can so easily be updated. For both of these reasons, preservation has seemed unnecessary. Moreover, modern librarianship rightly emphasizes service to users, rather than the mere accumulation of materials, as its primary professional concern. Instant access to information is regarded – at least by information providers – as the ideal and there is an implicit assumption that what is needed is the 'new' or up-to-date information, which is most likely to be contained in the most recent publications, in whatever physical form. Preservation of materials has been too easily dismissed as the esoteric concern of the archivist or the rare book librarian, of little or

1

no interest even in the mainstream of academic or public librarianship, let alone in the fashionable electronic world of information science.

The fundamental fallacy in this line of argument will be explored later, but we must begin by considering the concept of 'preservation' and defining some of the words which we shall be using. Three terms need to be clearly understood, and the distinction between them carefully maintained. These are:

* preservation
* conservation
* restoration.

Preservation is an aspect of the management of the library. Its objective is to ensure that information survives in an accessible and usable form for as long as it is wanted. In many cases, this implies its survival for the same period of time as the physical medium in which it is contained, such as a manuscript, a printed book, or a photograph. With audiovisual and electronic media, however, different considerations apply. These media – ranging from audio tape to multimedia CD-ROMs – are in some cases inherently unstable, but the information they contain can, without loss of quality, be replicated almost instantaneously and in multiple copies. The preservation of the original format is of little or no artistic or aesthetic interest (as might be the case with a manuscript or some printed books), and the preservation and accessibility of the information is actually improved by the creation of a new generation of copies. This fundamental difference, perhaps only recently coming to be fully recognised and articulated, will increasingly inform our understanding of how information preservation is to be achieved. Whatever methods may be used, the essential characteristic of preservation is that it is a large-scale operation, concerned with the effective management of the library's stock, or the information resource to which it has both local and distant access.

Conservation is one aspect of preservation activity. It normally implies the active use of preventative measures, or processes of repair of damaged material, to ensure the continued existence of individual items. Even here, however, there is an important managerial element. The decision on intervention – that is, the decision to repair a particular item – is essentially managerial or professional. The decision on the process and materials to be used may be technical, but even that has to be taken within the broad parameters of managerially determined policy. In the case of materials of historical importance, professional guidance and judgment are essential, but the librarian or archivist will work closely with (and seek the advice of) the conservator.

Restoration is the least common and in many ways the least useful of the three terms, for in this context it has a very precise meaning. It is taken to mean the attempt to restore a damaged item to its original condition by careful imitation of materials and techniques. Such an activity can, of course, be justified in aesthetic and historical terms; we do not repair medieval cathedrals with reinforced concrete (at least not in their visible parts): it would be equally insensitive to restore a medieval manuscript with a binding covered in imitation leather. In practice, the cost of restoration, and the use of the rare skills it demands, can be justified only in the very few cases of books of outstanding beauty or importance, whose significance as artefacts is at least as great as their significance as carriers of information. In general, it is a term perhaps best left to the world of art and architecture, and applied to library materials only where they, too, are 'works of art'.

A brief history

It has become conventional, at least among rare book librarians in Europe, to regard the Florence flood of 1966 as the beginning of the recent revival of interest in the preservation of books and documents. In the autumn of that year, the River Arno burst its banks in the middle of the city and caused devastating damage. Among the flooded buildings was the Biblioteca Nazionale, where nearly half a million books and manuscripts suffered from the inflow of water and mud. A huge international rescue effort was mounted by Unesco, with binders and conservators recruited from all over the

3

world to help in restoring the library's treasures. The sheer size of the problem they confronted forced them to develop new techniques for dealing with water-damaged paper and bookbindings. Some of these techniques, especially that of freeze-drying, have now become standard practice throughout the world. Moreover, since there were not enough trained personnel to cope with the work, a whole generation of conservators had to be trained at Florence, or were trained subsequently by those who learned their craft there. Florence was indeed a critical episode in the history of conservation and restoration. Old skills which might otherwise have been lost were handed on to a new generation, while the new techniques that were developed have proved invaluable elsewhere (Ogden 1979). In one sense, however, the response to the disaster at the Biblioteca Nazionale had a negative effect, for, in some eyes, it confirmed the traditional image of conservation: a matter for those concerned with rare books and manuscripts and, moreover, a craft-based activity dealing with individual books and documents whose practitioners were skilled, meticulous and inordinately slow.

The terrible damage wrought to one of Europe's great libraries was, however, only one theme in a much longer and more complex story. While some new techniques were developed by the international team at Florence, their basic skills were as old as bookbinding itself: they worked with vellum, parchment, paper, boards and leather; they repaired and restored, trying to achieve historical accuracy and verisimilitude; and where books were very badly damaged they tried to recreate an object sympathetic to the original. It was, for the most part, hand-craft work at the highest level. Because of the devastation, librarians became even more aware of the vulnerability of their collections.

There was, however, another source of the revived interest in preservation in the 1960s, and one which perhaps more accurately pointed the way to the future. The great research libraries of North America faced their own, very different, preservation problem. Although many of them have great collections of earlier material, they are, above all, libraries of 19th- and 20th-century books and documents. Even in the Library of Congress the legal deposit collections, which form the largest single group of its holdings, are, by definition, from the period since the Library was founded in 1800, and most of them indeed date from after the 1840s. Consequently, a very high proportion of the books in American research libraries are printed or written on paper dating from the worst period in the history of papermaking. (See also pp. 20–23.)

The basic problem the libraries confronted was a simple physical one: the decaying acidic paper had become embrittled, and could no longer be handled. Any pressure caused it to disintegrate and even on the shelves, without any handling at all, the paper was quietly deteriorating. The chemistry of paper, and the consequences of the use of acid in its manufacture, had been the subject of scientific investigation in the late 19th century (Irvine and Woodhead 1894), but by that time librarians were already observing some of the practical consequences (Johnson 1891). The work of Barrow and his colleagues from the 1930s onwards (Barrow 1959; Clapp 1972) brought together the findings of the scientists and the empirical observations and professional needs of the librarians. By that time, decaying paper was already a matter of concern to both British and American librarians (Library Association 1930; Jarrell 1936). The New York Public Library recognized the implications of the problem, and initiated a major programme to make microfilms of endangered books. This was quite different from the traditional concern of librarians to ensure that books were appropriately bound and that the bindings were kept in reasonable repair, a concern which antedates the organization of librarianship as a profession, and was a key area of professional debate during the late 19th century (Higginbotham 1990).

Even so, the full extent of the problem was not appreciated until the 1960s, when its scale was revealed in a series of surveys of major American libraries. The situation was at its worst in the industrial cities of the north-east and mid-west of the United States, but it was not good anywhere. At Columbia University in New York City it was estimated in 1975 that some 30% of the library's holdings of about five million items were embrittled (Battin 1985: 34); the corresponding figure at Berkeley, in the comparatively unpolluted atmosphere of the San Francisco Bay area, was 10% (Ogden 1985: 64-5). It was, however, at the Library of Congress and New York

Public Library that the position was worst. In the mid-1970s it was calculated that some six million of the former's seventeen million books were in an *advanced* stage of deterioration. At the New York Public, with its research collections housed in an ageing building in mid-town Manhattan, the figure was as high as 50%. It was suggested that in both libraries, all of the non-fiction published between 1900 and 1939 would be unusable by the end of the century (Library of Congress 1980: 14). This was the *real* preservation crisis, far greater in extent, if less likely to grab the headlines in the world's newspapers, than any damage caused by the Arno in Florence. A current estimate is that some 20% of the total contents of the world's libraries and archives is too badly decayed to be used (Rüttimann 1994).

It was clear that a problem on this scale required solutions that were quite different in degree and in kind from the traditional techniques of the craftsman conservator. Even the new methods developed in Florence, and indeed the new workers trained there, could not cope with the state of affairs revealed in the late 1960s and early 1970s. The traditional conservators were essentially trained to deal with books printed or written on handmade papers, and bound by hand using traditional methods and materials. Such work was as time-consuming as it was skilful, and could be used only for a tiny number of books. Temporary measures could indeed be used to prevent the further deterioration of damaged books, but such solutions as boxing could not cope with the millions of decaying items in the major American libraries. Even if a mass boxing programme could be funded and undertaken, the books would continue to decay inside the boxes. This was a fundamentally different problem from that of the typical 17th- or 18th-century book, where the conservator was normally confronted with a broken-down binding but paper that was essentially sound. What was now at stake was the text-block itself, and therefore the print it contained. It was 19th- and 20th-century materials, rather than those from earlier periods, which were now the centre of concern.

New directions

This called for a fundamental shift of emphasis in the planning and implementation of preservation programmes, a shift which took two directions:

- the scale and speed of the techniques used had to be appropriate to the size of the problem and the rapidity of its development
- the text and the information it contained rather than the book itself became the principal objective of preservation.

The sheer size of the problem of acidic and embrittled paper, especially in the United States, called for the development of mass techniques, which were not only different from those used by craftsman conservators but were also derived from a fundamentally different philosophy (Foot 1994). The meticulous treatment of individual items could no longer be seen as the salvation of the millions of books and documents that were now recognized to be in imminent danger not merely of damage but of total destruction. For those that had not yet disintegrated there was some possibility of rescue if the acidity which was the cause of their problems could be removed from the paper, or if its effects could be neutralized. A great deal of time and money was devoted to research into the deacidification of paper by the Library of Congress, the Council on Library Resources and other agencies in the United States and elsewhere.

The results have been encouraging. Working from the principle that a chemical problem needed a chemical solution, a number of deacidification processes have been developed. Some are successful in treating large numbers of books simultaneously. The capital costs are high, because the processes are designed to operate on a large scale, and therefore have to be carried out in industrial-sized plants if they are to be cost-effective. A number of such plants have been or are being built, for several different methods of deacidification. The size and cost inevitably mean that they are enterprises at a national or regional level, often with large infusions of public funding. National libraries dominate the move towards mass deacidification, since they alone can justify the costs and gain access to the funding. The Bibliothèque Nationale de France can treat some 4000 books per week; the Public Archives of Canada treats in the region of 40,000 items per year. The Library of Congress, coping with a problem on an unparalleled scale, intends to respond accordingly and continues to develop and evaluate processes (Harris and Shahani 1995). Other countries and institutions are also pursuing various techniques (see pp.118–121).

The preservation of the information content of a book or document, as opposed to the original physical format, is sometimes the only solution to preserving it at all, even with traditional paper-based media. In practice, this has normally meant the creation of so-called 'surrogates', in which the information is recorded in another medium but in its original visual form. Until very recently, this could be achieved only by photography, and the normal surrogate medium was 35 mm microfilm, although microfiches were also used. Preservation microfilming has been undertaken since the 1930s, when it was pioneered at the New York Public Library. Indeed, it marked the beginning of that institution's response to its recognition of its massive preservation problem. It has subsequently become a widespread practice, to the extent of becoming the normal means of ensuring the availability of long runs of newspapers and journals, as well as the contents of decaying books. In the United States, although not in Europe, it is not uncommon for the original to be abandoned once the master negative has been made, so that the film becomes the only source of the data (see pp.121–123).

It has been recognized for more than a decade that electronic storage systems are potentially a very attractive alternative to film as surrogate media. Digitization is now a working technique, which is increasingly able to produce acceptable output. The issues raised by digitization, and the related but separate issue of the preservation of data that has never existed in other than digital form, are the main subject of Chapter Three of this book, but some basic principles and distinctions are needed at this stage (see pp.51–77).

First, we have to distinguish between storage media and output media. It seems likely that the optical disc (or CD) will be the principal form of output and consultation for the foreseeable future, at least as far as surrogates are concerned. It can record both the information content and the visual appearance of the text in the original book or document; in other words, it has the qualities that made film an acceptable surrogate medium, while having the additional benefit of far more powerful retrieval methods. This does not mean, however, that such disks are themselves suitable for long-term preservation of information. Indeed, their long-term survival properties have not yet been fully established. Optical discs, therefore, have to be seen as a medium for consultation rather than for permanent storage.

The second general point follows from this: the storage medium of digitized data must be permanent and stable, or steps must be taken to avoid the consequences of instability. When this principle is accepted, two further problems present themselves. First, systems are rapidly superseded because of the speed of development of new systems. The supersession of one system by another is hardly the ideal circumstance in which to create surrogates designed for permanent preservation. A number of electronic media are already obsolete, and the equipment on which to run them is no longer generally available. Secondly, storage of electronic data is unstable and invisible. Because of the inherent instability of the magnetic medium itself, and its susceptibility to electronic and physical damage, as well as the impossibility of visual observation of such damage, it is necessary to copy the data store at regular intervals if the preservation of the data is to be guaranteed. This concept of "refreshment" is central to the use of electronic storage for long-term information preservation. These considerations apply whether electronic media are used as surrogates for printed and written documents, analogously with the use of photographic methods since before World War II, or whether an attempt is to be made to preserve data that has never taken printed or written form.

Mass deacidification and mass surrogacy programmes have been two of the most potent and effective responses to the preservation crisis, and in particular to the problems posed by the embrittlement of acidic paper. Both are in origin American solutions to what was first seen as an American problem, although both have been applied successfully in Europe and elsewhere in the world. Neither, however, is a total solution to the preservation problem, and indeed their advocates would not make such a claim. The issue has a far wider dimension; in particular there is a growing acceptance of the need to take preventive measures, which will ensure that the present crisis will not recur in the future, or will at least have the effect of reducing it to a manageable size. This is particularly important as we come to rely more and more on electronic information, stored in a computer and delivered to the end user over a network or on optical disc. Preservation managers will inevitably need to be increasingly concerned with this matter, not merely because it may offer some new and potent solutions to old problems, but because it is creating wholly new ones of its own.

Perhaps the most important single development in the preservation field in the last 20 years has been the recognition of the universality of the problem, even before the electronic dimension was added to it. Decaying newspapers, uniquely, are as likely to be found in the local studies section of a public library as they are in some great national repository. All libraries have a problem if the majority of the books and journals they buy have a built-in obsolescence of little more than two or three decades, or their structure is so poor that the binding will not survive even two years of normal use. Rising prices and falling budgets have forced librarians to reconsider the rate of redundancy and replacement of stock, while the continuous growth of the publishing industry places ever increasing demands on those same diminishing budgets. More books and less money means that those books that are selected have to have been chosen more carefully before they are bought, and cherished more effectively after they have been acquired. The selection and management of the stock has become a live issue in librarianship during the last decade of economic stringency, to a far greater extent than it ever was during the expansive decades after World War II. The economic aspect of the problem is perhaps at its most acute in the United Kingdom, where public funding of libraries is most widespread. Britain's vast network of public libraries, unparalleled anywhere in the world, is entirely dependent for its budget upon the vagaries of central and local government policy. Moreover, in Britain, unlike the United States, virtually the entire academic library system is also publicly funded, either directly or indirectly. The continuous financial pressure on public sector budgets since 1979 has inevitably meant that almost all public and academic libraries have suffered severe cuts in real terms to their budgets, since the increases in book funds have never kept pace with the rate of price inflation. Stocks, and indeed services, have suffered, and the need to preserve stock has become ever more obvious, especially as the quality of service provision tends to be specially protected.

Preservation in Britain

It is against this background that we have to consider the British approach to preservation, which has been distinctively different from that of the Americans; naturally enough, it reflects circumstances in the United Kingdom just as the American approach reflects those in the United States. During the late 1970s, the British Library gradually came to recognize the extent of its own conservation problem; its growing awareness and its increasingly sophisticated responses can be traced through successive annual reports. In its very first report, in 1974, the British Library Board announced that it was 'deeply concerned about the problem of conservation', a sentiment which it repeated ('great concern') in the following year. In 1975 a Conservation Branch was established, which during the next five years developed an active, but conventional, policy for the care of the stock. Substantial funds were made available for conservation, but they seem to have been devoted largely to the repair of individual items. A survey of the collections, however, revealed that the British Library's problem, although different from that of the Library of Congress, was in some ways just as great. Two centuries of neglect, not always benign, had left some of the collections in a parlous condition. A century of storage in overcrowded and badly ventilated bookstacks in the heart of a polluted city had not helped. Finally, vastly increased use since 1945 had completed the process of creating the perfect circumstances for large-scale and serious damage.

As a consequence, resources had to be redirected. In 1979-80, for the first time, expenditure on conservation exceeded that on acquisitions and by the early 1980s the Conservation Branch was involved in a 'sustained campaign for the care of books among staff and readers', in the creation of microform surrogates, and in research on deacidification. By the late 1980s a further survey had revealed that some 14% of the Library's post-1850 books were on embrittled paper, yet again emphasizing the sheer scale of the problem. In 1988-9, the Humanities and Social Sciences Division (the former Reference Division) spent nearly £5.5m on preservation. However, even the neutral prose of the Board's annual reports cannot conceal a distinct change in philosophy in the early 1980s. In 1983-4, the Conservation Branch was replaced by a Preservation Service, and began to put ever more emphasis on mass preservation, especially microform surrogate programmes. Cheaper processes of boxing and rebinding, and what the report for 1986-7 rather coyly called 'greater emphasis on lower-cost options', became the main thrust of the Library's policy, while it also began to play a more active role in the identification and partial solution of preservation problems on a national scale. This included funding the first major national study of preservation in British libraries (Ratcliffe 1984), support for a survey of preservation management in the education of librarians (Feather and Lusher 1989) and an important contribution to scientific developments in both photographic and digital technologies (Hendley 1983) and paper strengthening (Clements, Butler and Millington 1988; Foot 1995).

During the same ten or fifteen years, the other national libraries of the United Kingdom made equally alarming discoveries about the state of their stocks and the cost of remedying the problems. Again, annual reports provide eloquent testimony. The National Library of Scotland estimated in 1986 that 15– 20% of its stock was in need of active intervention if it was to be preserved. A budget of £600,000 per year had been allocated, but the Library's preservation manager was far from complacent about the level of activity. Two years later the budget had not increased. The situation in Wales is comparable; preservation activity has increased at the National Library but, as elsewhere, cannot match the scale of the problem (Rees 1988).

It is against this background that the Ratcliffe Report has to be understood. This document, published in 1984, can now be seen as a turning-point in the definition and understanding of library preservation in the United Kingdom. Its methodology, and hence its findings, reflect the preoccupations of British librarians – and especially those of the senior managers of the Reference Division of the British Library – in the early 1980s. It was essentially a survey of attitudes and opinions, and it revealed alarming ignorance and perhaps equally alarming naïvety about the preservation issue itself and the solutions that were available. An astonishing 162 out of 332 libraries that responded to a questionnaire (about 80% of those circulated) declared their intention to retain between 81 and 100% of their stock 'permanently'. Yet only 9 libraries actually had a written preservation policy statement! Staff training in conservation was minimal everywhere and non-existent in 189 libraries. The subject had all but vanished from the curricula of the library schools, and only 36 libraries offered even the most basic preservation awareness training to their staff. The gap between intention and practice suggested that few British library managers had given any real thought to the implications of their traditional instinct for permanent retention of the entire stock. This was, perhaps, especially true in the university sector and in the major urban public libraries. Ratcliffe's findings were to exercise a seminal influence on developments in Britain for the rest of the 1980s.

The need for training and education to remedy the general ignorance of the preservation issue was one of Ratcliffe's principal recommendations. There is evidence that this had some effect. In particular, there has been an emphasis on in-service training for practitioners, on the teaching in library schools of preservation management to new entrants to the profession, and on the inclusion of preservation awareness in induction courses for non-professional staff and in user education programmes. Quite apart from the important developments in the library schools, academic libraries in particular have responded to the situation Ratcliffe revealed. By 1986 there was already a slight improvement, if only in the sense that nearly 50% of librarians claimed to have been influenced by Ratcliffe's findings (Mowat 1987: 38). In 1988 it was found that 17 out of 53 member libraries of the Standing Committee on National and University Libraries (SCONUL) (a 76% response) had a written preservation policy (compared with Ratcliffe's finding of 2), and the number of full-time and presumably expert conservation officers had doubled from 12 to 24. Nine additional institutions (to Ratcliffe's 20) had systematically conducted preservation surveys of their stock, and 19 (as against 2) had prepared a disaster plan (Moon and Loveday 1989). At this level, therefore, it is clear that some British academic libraries responded rapidly and positively to the preservation crisis once it was identified. If public libraries were less immediately responsive, it was at least partly because they have so many other calls on even more limited funds and staffing. In some quarters, there was enthusiasm, knowledge and commitment (Beard 1987).

The first comprehensive national study since Ratcliffe, carried out exactly ten years later with financial support from the Leverhulme Foundation, revealed a more mixed picture than some of the more optimistic visions of the middle and late 1980s (Feather, Matthews and Eden 1996). There was a greater awareness of preservation as an issue than Ratcliffe had found, but a decade during which library budgets in all sectors had been under almost continuous pressure had left its mark. Moreover, there was still a clear tendency to identify preservation with rare books and manuscripts rather than to associate it with the broader issues of information access. The Leverhulme study, however, provided the occasion for the initiation of a wider debate on national policies, in which preservation, retention and access were coming to be seen as a single spectrum of issues rather than existing in discrete compartments. (National Preservation Office [forthcoming]).

The large-scale surveys undertaken by Ratcliffe in the early 1980s and by Eden, Matthews and Feather in the early 1990s provide a context for an understanding of the large and growing descriptive literature on preservation in libraries of all kinds. Much of this literature offers valuable insights into the problem as perceived by practitioners. Of course, every library has its own unique problems, but the recurrence of certain themes in the literature and in the findings of the Leverhulme study suggests that there are also some areas of shared interest, even between apparently very different institutions. The physical causes of the preservation problem are common to all libraries, archives and information agencies.

Information cannot exist in a permanent form unless it is stored in some medium. All the information media have a physical base, whether paper or vinyl or celluloid. If the physical base is lost then the information held on it is also lost.

That apparently simple statement is the fundamental issue of preservation. In the past, even the very recent past, it could have been expressed in a slightly different way: to transmit the message, we have to preserve the medium. Perhaps the most truly radical development of the last decade is that we now have to modify that expression, for we have information storage methods in which the data can actually be preserved more easily than an essentially transient medium and system (Buchanan and Jensen 1995; Speller 1994). The need to preserve such data, and the use of such systems for the preservation of information originally disseminated in a different physical format, is an issue which cannot be ignored if the entire range of preservation issues and their implications is to be fully explored.

We must not, however, neglect the wider context. The same physical faults that are the root cause of the preservation problem make it impossible, even if it were desirable, to preserve everything everywhere. Archivists have always recognized the need for selectivity. They accept the unpalatable truth that 'some records will have to be left to decay' (Thomas 1983: 177) and a similar attitude will have to be developed by librarians, including those who see themselves primarily as custodians of the heritage. To preserve information, it may even be necessary to sacrifice the original medium, and in some cases the medium can be sacrificed without loss. Even for traditional materials, the complex and expensive techniques of restoration can never be justified for more than a tiny minority of books and manuscripts.

The essence of the matter is, therefore, selectivity. Selection, however, would be pointless if it were random. It is therefore necessary to have criteria to help to determine the priority of each case. To develop a policy that will define those criteria it is necessary to understand the physical facts which make the policy necessary in the first place. For that reason, a librarian needs to know something of the physical basis of books and other media. Nevertheless, a knowledge of the chemistry of paper or the technique of case-binding is not to be confused with an understanding of preservation. In the last analysis, preservation policy consists of a series of decisions determined by considerations of organization and finance as well as by the use and contents of the library, and in our networked world can no longer be seen solely in the context of a single institution or even a single country. Preservation is expensive. If it is to be more than the temporary repair of randomly selected items, an informed and agreed policy is needed. The preservation problem has a physical cause, but its solution can come only from good, effective and well-informed management.

Further reading

There is now an extensive literature on preservation, both for beginners and for more advanced students and practitioners. Important introductory works include Harvey (1993) and Swartzburg (1995). For the development of preservation policies and practices in the USA since the early 1960s, see Darling and Ogden (1981). For the UK, the Ratcliffe Report (Ratcliffe 1984) remains the key document, although for a fuller understanding of the position in the mid-1990s, and of the influence (and failures) of Ratcliffe, the Leverhulme study must be consulted (Feather, Matthews and Eden, 1995).

Chapter 2
MEDIA, MATERIALS AND THE ENVIRONMENT

The materials of information storage

Preservation has vast financial and organizational implications, which will be explored in Chapters 4, 5 and 6. However, as we have seen, there would be no problem if the materials on which we store information were not subject to damage and decay. Damage, whether by human agency or by other means, can be avoided to some extent, and certainly provisions can be made to minimize its consequences if it should happen by accident. Decay, however, is intrinsic to all the materials used for information storage both now and in the past. To understand the need for preservation, and the methods by which it can be achieved, it is therefore necessary to begin with an understanding of the nature of information storage materials, and the defects inherent in them. In this chapter, we shall consider the traditional materials – the constituents of books and manuscripts – and also photographic materials. In Chapter 3, we shall turn to the issues which arise from the use of electronic formats.

Book materials

Paper

Paper is the most common medium on which information is recorded. It is still and has been since before the invention of printing, and indeed most of what has been stored in written or printed form is available only on paper. Some knowledge of the history and properties of paper, and of the papermaking process is, therefore, the necessary starting-point for the study and practice of preservation.

The Chinese invented paper in the second century AD; it gradually made its way westwards during the next four hundred years following the ancient trade routes of central Asia. The use of paper, and the knowledge of the papermaking process, reached the Middle East at about the time of the great Arab conquests of the seventh and eighth centuries. It was through the subsequent Arab incursions across the Mediterranean that paper and papermaking first reached southern Europe, in Sicily, Spain and Italy. By the 13th century it was in widespread use, to the extent that when printing was invented in the middle of the 15th century, paper was being manufactured in considerable quantities throughout southern and western Europe. The materials it displaced – parchment and vellum – continued in use for some time, but paper had become the normal medium for written documents by the middle of the 16th century at the latest, and printed books were rarely produced on anything else.

The basic constituent of paper is fibrous vegetable matter. This need not be taken directly from the plant, since vegetable fibres that have already been processed and manufactured can be recycled for use in papermaking. Indeed, paper itself can be used in this way, and frequently is; cheaper papers are almost invariably made by recycling used paper of a higher quality. Recycling has become even more common in recent years, with our growing concern about the rate at which we are consuming the earth's natural resources. The fibres can also, however, be taken from other products, such as natural fabrics, especially linen and cotton cloth. The strength and durability of the paper ultimately depends upon the quality of the matter from which it is made, and the processes and chemicals used in papermaking.

The method of papermaking invented by the Chinese was an entirely hand-craft process. Essentially the same techniques continued to be used in the west without significant change until the beginning of the 19th century . Indeed, even today some paper is still made by traditional hand methods, as a hobby in the west and for commercial papers (although not for ordinary printing) in some south-east Asian countries. In the process of hand papermaking the first stage is to break down the vegetable matter, in whatever form, into its constituent fibres; this process was partially mechanized in the 17th century when a machine called a *Hollander* was designed in which the material was torn into pulp by blades under a steady flow of water. The result of this process is a thick liquid pulp, known to papermakers as *stuff*, to which various other substances may then be added. These additives include: a size to seal the surface of the paper, for otherwise all paper would be absorbent like blotting paper; dyes, if coloured paper is being made; or bleach, if the fibres and the water being used will not give the paper a sufficiently 'white' appearance.

The stuff is picked out of the vat in which it has been made by means of a rectangular wooden frame called a *mould*. The longer side of the mould can be comfortably held in the hands of a person with arms outstretched. Lengths of wire, at intervals of approximately 2 cm, run parallel to the shorter sides along the whole length of the mould. Parallel to the longer sides, and at much closer intervals (ideally of about 1 mm) run much thinner wires. The former are called *chains* and the latter *wires*. Sewn into them may be a pattern of wires which forms the papermaker's trade mark; this is called the *watermark*. The papermaker also has a second, slightly larger, wooden frame called the *deckle*, with no chains or wires. The deckle fits snugly over the mould but has slightly protruding edges. When the papermaker dips the mould into the vat he picks up enough stuff to spread across the porous surface formed by the chains and wires. He shakes off any surplus water, and then puts the deckle on to the mould before shaking it again. Finally, he removes the deckle and turns out the sheet of still wet, but now solidifying, stuff on to a sheet of felt. The felt absorbs the excess moisture, and the stuff dries into a sheet of paper. Another piece of felt is immediately placed on top of the sheet, and then the next sheet from the mould on top of that, and so on, until a pile of several hundred sheets of paper and felt has been formed. This is pressed to squeeze out any remaining water. When the paper has lost all its moisture, the felt is removed and the drying process is then complete.

It is the chains, wires and watermark which enable us to identify paper made by this method. Where the stuff lies over them in the mould, the sheet is slightly thinner than it is elsewhere. Consequently, *chain lines*, *wire lines* and an impression of the watermark are formed where the paper is also a little thinner. If a sheet of hand-made paper is held up to the light, they are clearly visible. Some modern machine-made papers have artificial watermarks. However, few papers likely to be found in libraries or archives have artificial chain-lines, so their presence is a very reliable indicator that the paper is hand-made.

Until the end of the 18th century, most western papers were made from linen rags. Such paper was of a very high quality, with a good general appearance and, most importantly, a high tensile strength. The stuff needed little by way of chemical additives to prepare it for use, and the paper itself was suitable for both writing and printing. It had to be sized so that ink would adhere to the surface, but little more was done to it. By the late 18th century, however, there was a serious problem; the demand for paper was increasing, both for printing and for other purposes. At the same time, the supply of linen rags was diminishing as cotton replaced it as the cheapest fabric. Although cotton rags can be used for papermaking, they produce poor paper. To compensate for lower-quality materials, papermakers began to use chlorine bleaches and other additives to provide the colour and strength their customers demanded. In itself, this was only a temporary solution; in the end, the papermakers had to find new methods and new materials to satisfy the insatiable demand for their product. Thus began a decline in the quality of paper which was not to be arrested for more than a century.

One of the long-term solutions to the problem of increased demand lay in the invention of a method of papermaking, other than the slow traditional method of hand manufacture. The papermaking machine was invented by a Frenchman, Nicholas-Louis Robert, in 1796, but in those unpropitious times, he could find no backers in his own country, and so took himself and his designs to England. There he attracted the financial support of the brothers Henry and Sealy Fourdrinier, who owned a wholesale stationery business in London. In 1806, the first working machine was built; it was named after its patrons rather than its inventor.

The basic principle upon which the Fourdrinier machine depended continues to be used in its modern successors. Fibres are pushed into the machine, and the stuff mechanically beaten, at one (the *wet*) end. The stuff then flows from the vat on to a conveyor belt, where it is thinned to paper thickness, and dried out, either naturally or by jets of hot air. It emerges at the other (the *dry*) end as a continuous roll (*web*) of paper which can be cut to the desired length, or divided into single sheets. The process is simple and effective, but it requires a much greater use of chemicals than does hand papermaking, as well as artificial drying mechanisms. The early machines produced paper that was acceptable to its immediate users but whose long-term survival properties were significantly fewer than those of its hand-made, and largely unadulterated, predecessor.

In the long term, the changes in the technology of papermaking were to be of lesser significance for preservation than were the changes in the paper's constituent materials. Throughout the 19th century, there was a search for new, and preferably cheaper, substances that would be easily available to papermakers as a substitute for the decreasing supply of increasingly expensive rags. For the first time, paper was made of raw vegetable matter not previously subjected to a manufacturing process. There were various experiments with reeds and grasses in the 1840s and 1850s, but the final solution, and one which is still employed today, was the use of wood. Pulp made from wood fulfilled all the basic requirements of the 19th-century papermakers in terms of its cost and availability. In northern Europe and North America there were apparently unlimited quantities of it in great forests which were still largely unexploited. Two methods of pulping were invented; both are still in use. The first produces *mechanical wood* paper, by simply tearing apart the whole of the log, after the bark has been stripped away, and using water to convert it into pulp. This produces the very cheap but not particularly durable paper used, for example, for newspapers and paperbacks. The second process produces *chemical wood* paper. In this method, chemicals are used to catalyse changes in the molecular structure of the pulp. The effect is to produce a 'whiter' and visually more attractive paper of the sort used for writing and for book printing. Chemical wood paper is also more durable than mechanical wood paper, although it is far from perfect when compared with good linen-rag papers (Priest 1987: 165). However, the process of turning trees into paper is quick, cheap and simple. The paper that was thus created in the 19th century was destined to be a major cause of one of the most important aspects of the preservation crisis in the libraries of the world a century later, when acidic and embrittled papers turned to dust.

The fundamental problem is that wood-based paper, whether mechanical or chemical, is naturally high in acidity. The lignin, one of its chemical constituents, oxidizes in contact with the air; other chemicals present react badly to light. The details need not detain us, but the consequences are crucial. In general terms, it is true to say that paper with a high acid content will decay naturally and irreversibly over a comparatively short period of time. For over a century, from the 1860s onwards, the great majority of European and American books were printed on acidic paper. Acidic paper was used for written (and later typewritten) documents. Bookbinders used it as a matter of course for endpapers and labels. Because the problem was not generally understood, no steps were taken to prevent or circumvent it until the 1970s, so that the most basic material of information storage and preservation was inherently unstable, without the majority of its users or even its custodians even being aware of the fact.

The scientific study of paper began in the late 19th century, but it was not until the 1930s that standards for 'permanent' paper were first considered (Burton 1931). It was, of course, at the same time that the problem of embrittlement, which is the most significant manifestation of the chemical decay of paper, was being identified in some American libraries. Even then progress was painfully slow. The pioneering work of the paper scientists at last bore fruit in an American standard for permanent paper in 1985, and such paper now seems to be widely used (American National Standards Institute 1984). As yet no similar standard has been adopted in the United Kingdom. The Library Association and The Publishers' Association have reached a broad measure of agreement on the subject, but the 'standard' cannot be enforced, although the use of 'acid-free' (i.e. chemically inert) paper is becoming more common.

From the perspective of the librarian or the archivist, the manifestations and immediate triggers of the decay of paper are perhaps more important than the scientific details of its ultimate causes. Decay caused by a high acid content is most easily identified by the fact that the paper browns and becomes brittle. Eventually the paper will disintegrate completely, even without being touched. It has to be emphasized that this process takes place even in environmental conditions that are broadly favourable to paper storage. As we shall see, such conditions rarely exist in major libraries, and the process of decay is therefore exacerbated. The world's libraries and archives are in fact full of documents written and printed on wood-pulp paper that will gradually turn to dust even if they are never used, as the preservation surveys of the last 20 years have so dramatically revealed.

Decay is inherent in the materials of many machine-made papers. There is an additional hazard common to all papers, even those that are chemically stable or inert: because the papermaking process consists of first wetting and then drying the materials, it follows that the wetness or dryness of the paper is critical to its survival. In very dry conditions, paper loses its essential remaining moisture, and becomes brittle. If it is too damp, however, the papermaking process itself is partly reversed, and the paper will begin to disintegrate.

Parchment

Parchment, or vellum (the difference is irrelevant for our purposes), is treated animal skin which can be used for binding or, more frequently, as a writing surface. The skins of sheep, goats and cattle were all used for this purpose. Parchment was first used as a writing material in the middle of the second millennium BC in Egypt, and continued in regular use until the late Middle Ages in western Europe. Indeed, its use for certain legal documents, such as wills, survived the invention of printing. However, it was rarely used for printed books; not only was it far more expensive than paper, even in the 15th century, it was also very difficult to print a good impression on its slightly uneven surface. Nevertheless, parchment is, after paper, the substance most commonly found in archives and manuscript collections.

Parchment is prepared by washing the animal skin in water, scraping off the hair and treating the skin with lime; it is not tanned. The skin is then dried at normal temperatures, but under tension on a specially made stretching frame. The result is a material with a very high tensile strength and reasonably resilient provided it is kept dry. Like paper, it will degrade very rapidly if it is damp, because it can absorb large amounts of water quickly, which has the effect of reversing the drying stage of the manufacturing process. Parchment is a stiff substance, far less flexible than leather, but for a writing surface, especially when it is folded and bound, this is of course an advantage. In general, parchment documents survive at least as well as those on paper, and indeed good parchment is probably more durable than the cheap printing and writing papers of the last 150 years.

Leather

The pages of a bound book – the *text-block* – are, of course, normally protected by a binding. As we shall see, the structural basis of a bookbinding is that the protective outer cover is linked in some way to the text-block. The critical factors in determining the survival properties of a binding are therefore the qualities of the materials used and the strength of the linkage between the book and its cover. Like paper, bookbinding materials have chemical and physical characteristics that are crucially significant for preservation.

Until the beginning of the 19th century, bookbindings were made completely by hand, using organic materials. The boards were made in the same way and from the same materials as paper. The whole construction was covered in treated animal skin, normally calf's leather, although sometimes sheepskin, goatskin or some other material was used. However, from the early 19th century, leather began to be displaced by cloths made of natural fibres, such as cotton and linen.

Leather-covered bookbindings are typical of all collections of books dating from before the early 19th century, and indeed for some bindings leather was in use long after the development of bookcloths. The quality of leather, like that of paper, depends largely on the manufacturing process. In leather manufacture, the cleaned skin is tanned, that is to say treated with alkaline chemicals which strengthen it, make it flexible and give it a shiny appearance on the inner (or *flesh*) side. This appearance can be enhanced by subsequent polishing with wax or oils. Good leathers are exceedingly durable, and can survive heavy usage for centuries, but inadequate tanning with poor chemicals will produce leather with little strength.

As in the case of papermaking, the need to meet increased demand led to the use of tanning agents whose product was less durable than their earlier equivalents. This decline began at a much earlier date than that of paper. From the mid-17th century onwards, leathers were made that tended to crumble and rot if continuously exposed to certain environmental conditions, especially heat or sunlight. By the middle of the 19th century, poor-quality leathers were almost the norm for bookbinding work. Unfortunately, this coincided with a period when many great libraries were organizing the unsorted accumulations of decades or centuries, and the binding programmes which were part of this process made use of very poor, and now badly decayed, leather.

These poor leathers will dry out and turn to a powdery dust if they are consistently too hot, as they are in glass-fronted bookcases exposed to the sun, for example, a situation typical of so many country-house libraries in 18th- and 19th-century England. If storage conditions are damp, the leather may not suffer too badly, but the boards themselves will hydrate and decay, as indeed will the paper. In either case, the result is the same: the binding disintegrates, and is likely to collapse completely when the book is handled. Millions of leather-bound books have lost one board or both, or have split hinges and joints, not because of careless handling but because of the inherent weakness of the materials from which they were made.

Bookcloths
The early 19th-century bookcloths, made of high-quality cotton fibre, were in general more satisfactory than much contemporary bookbinding leather. Although cheap cloths do decay, and react particularly badly to damp conditions, they are, for the most part,

very stable. The weakness of many 19th- and early 20th-century bindings lies not in the cloth, but in the acidic boards the cloth covers and in the acidic paper used for the endpapers and spine strips. Modern synthetic polymer 'cloths', while they are not always aesthetically very pleasing, do have a chemical stability denied to many of their organic predecessors.

Adhesives

Synthetic polymers have also largely replaced organic substances in the adhesives used in bookbinding. Traditionally, binders used either water based paste made from wheat- or rice-flour starches, or glue made from animal derivatives. Pastes are particularly suitable for bookbinding purposes, and indeed many modern conservators will use little else. The animal glues are more problematic; they tend to dry out and become inflexible and will then split when the book is opened. Moreover, some of them are, apparently, regarded as a treat by gourmandizing insects.

Book structures

The structure of the book is as important to its capacity to survive as is the quality of the materials from which it is made. Since about the fourth century AD, virtually all western, and western-influenced, books have been made in the familiar form of the *codex*, in which folded and sewn sheets are protected by an outer covering to which they are attached. Scrolls and rolls, the earlier methods of book construction, survived residually for certain archival purposes, for example the long rolls of parchment which form some medieval English records such as the Pipe Rolls of Exchequer, as well as in the consciously archaic use for copies of the Jewish scriptures for liturgical purposes. For all normal purposes, however, it is the codex structure with which we are concerned.

Until the late 19th century, the normal method of bookbinding, now called *craft binding*, created a strong physical link between the text-block and the outer cover. The sheets were folded and put into the correct order (*collated*), in a series of *gatherings*, each of which consisted of a number of leaves (from 2 to as many as 32), one inside the other. The gatherings were then sewn. The sewing method changed somewhat over the centuries, but the essence remained the same. A single piece of cotton or linen thread was used for the whole book. It was passed in and out of the centre of each gathering in turn, so that the gathering was held together internally. It was then passed through to the next gathering; the gatherings were thus linked to each other. Between each gathering, in what was to become the spine of the book, it was passed around much thicker cords, or *thongs*, to give added strength. These thongs were, in due course, passed through holes in the boards and secured there by knots or wedges, to link the text-block and the cover. Before that was done, however, the text-block itself was beaten with a special hammer along the spine, to give it the rounded shape which is necessary for proper opening of the book; in the same process (*rounding and backing*), recesses were created into which the boards could be placed to form hinges. Endpapers were sewn on to the text-block. Finally, the spine was strengthened and the boards and spine were covered with leather or some other material. The endpapers were pasted down inside the boards, over the knots and wedges at the ends of the sewing thongs. Sometimes the binder left a *free endpaper* (i.e. the leaf of the endpaper which is not pasted to the board) between the pastedown and the first leaf of the book itself. The result was a structure of great internal strength, supported by both the sewing and the adhesives.

Craft binding techniques are still used in conservation and restoration work, and very occasionally for expensive special editions, but for most purposes other techniques have inevitably displaced them. Almost all hardback books are now *case bound*. In this process, the text-block and the outer cover, or *case,* are made separately, and brought together only at the last moment. The text-block is sewn, trimmed, and rounded and backed. The endpapers are then attached by means of a thin strip of adhesive, rather than being sewn on. In addition, the spine is strengthened with a piece of strong paper, and with a piece of linen which protrudes a little beyond the edge of the book; the latter is called the *mull.* The case is machine-made, and consists simply of two boards and a slightly stiffened spine strip, all brought together by being glued to the covering material, normally cloth or some artificial fabric. The endpapers and the mull are then glued to the boards, and the book is complete. Almost the entire process of collation, binding, case-making and casing-in is mechanized, and is almost invariably used for binding the whole print-run of a book, since it is, in effect, a mass-production process.

A third technique, and one widely used for the binding of periodicals or for the rebinding of damaged books, is called *library binding*. Unlike case-binding, this is not a mass-production process, since individual and differing items are being bound. As a consequence, it offers some of the strengths of traditional craft techniques. In particular, the sewing threads are used to link the text-block and the outer covering, although that covering is really a case rather than the traditional boards.

Finally we should note the so-called *perfect binding*, a term which describes the precise opposite of this unfortunate technique. The sheets are collated and folded in the usual way, but are then guillotined a millimetre or so in from the fold. The text-block thus becomes a series of single sheets. The outer cover is attached to the 'spine' by adhesives applied under heat and pressure. The resulting 'book' will usually hold together long enough to be sold, but will rarely survive a single reading. This technique is the normal means of binding mass-market paperbacks in the United States. Such books are unsuitable for long-term use, and certainly not for permanent preservation in libraries, although some better techniques are now available. Unfortunately, it is impossible to rebind them conventionally because the gutter through which the sewing thread normally passes has been destroyed. The binder is, therefore, forced to use a technique called *stab binding* in which the thread passes through the single sheets at a right angle. It is inelegant, and unsatisfactory for large books, although it has historical precedents, having been used for pamphlets in the 17th and 18th centuries. It should be added that British and European paperback publishers rarely offend by using perfect bindings. Their products normally have sewn text-blocks which are attached to the outer cover by adhesive at the spine. When good paper and adhesives are used, this creates a surprisingly durable product.

The alternative solution to binding single sheets, often used for archival documents or single printed sheets of historical importance (such as proclamations or broadside ballads) is *guarding*. A guard book is a library-bound case, with stubs of paper rather than a text-block. The sheets are then glued to the stubs by a thin line of adhesive, and an unexpectedly strong book is thus created.

A bookbinding is a mechanical device. It is designed both to protect the text-block and to give access to it. Access can be achieved only by opening the book, which means the binding has to be flexible. Ideally, it should allow the book to lie open flat, without any pressure being exerted upon it and without any damage taking place. Some craft bindings achieve this ideal, but they are few, and almost no binding made by any other technique can approach it. A binding is mechanically most vulnerable at the hinges, upon which the boards turn. These are subject to great pressure, so that even in normal and careful use they may eventually break. Careless use, or inferior materials, will hasten their end. In a case-binding, the strength of the hinge ultimately depends on the covering material, since it alone links the boards and the spine.

In a craft-bound book, the hinge is, of course, further supported by the cords or thongs, and it is not unusual to see such a book in which the leather has cracked, but the cords are still holding the boards on to the text-block. In case-bound, and to a slightly lesser extent library-bound, books, the strength of the whole structure ultimately depends upon the adhesives, and where inferior adhesives are used, or storage conditions are wrong, the structure can collapse.

Non-book materials

Books are, of course, only one part of the contents of almost all libraries. The printed word has been produced in scores of different physical forms. Each presents its own problems to the librarian seeking to preserve it. Periodicals, for example, are typically issued without permanent bindings, and yet many libraries wish to preserve them in perpetuity. At least that is not inconsistent with the purpose their publisher had in mind. The same is not true of newspapers, where the librarian is seeking to preserve what is an essentially ephemeral product, with a life-expectancy of less than 24 hours and often produced on correspondingly poor paper. The multifarious forms of print – sheet music, maps, posters and many others – all have their place in the library, and for research libraries that seek to maintain comprehensive collections they present a serious and growing problem. They are produced on the same inherently unstable material as books and journals, and yet in some cases, unlike them, are not even designed for permanent preservation.

Archivists have to cope with even more diverse forms of documents than do librarians. Typing paper, for example, is usually of a fairly poor quality, and yet the 'manuscripts' of many modern literary works exist only in that form. So do millions of letters and other documents worthy of preservation. Even worse is the 'bank' paper which was used for carbon copies, found in almost all archival collections of modern documents. In the early years of typing, and indeed until after World War II, the quality of the carbon paper itself was also poor, so that legibility, let alone survival, becomes a serious problem. Some carbon images can be erased merely by contact. Photocopies, which have to a large extent displaced carbon copies, are equally problematic. Copies on plain paper, such as are now common, are probably fairly durable, but the early wet-copy processes used paper that decays rapidly and they produced an image which, in many cases, has already faded.

Computer printout is also to be found in some archival collections. Again, paper quality, especially of the 'listing paper' used in most continuous-feed printers, is poor, and the quality of the image weak. Such printout is really intended to be temporary, but if it is of archival interest it will have to be preserved in some form. In practice, however, large electronic files will be preserved by a wholly different strategy (see pp.51–77).

Non-printed materials

The printed word is still by far the most important means of information storage and seems likely to continue to be so for the foreseeable future. However, it has never been the only medium. Print itself never entirely displaced manuscript, and it is itself now being supplemented and partially replaced by photographic and electronic systems. In so far as these 'new' media (several of them actually more than a century old!) contain unique information not stored in printed form, they too will have to be preserved in some way as part of our information resource. Each of them presents its own range of problems, in many cases far more complex than those of print and paper.

Photographic media

Almost all libraries contain some photographic material. This takes many forms: cine films, slides, microforms, prints and so on. All of them have some common chemical characteristics which partly determine their ability to survive. Photographic film and paper are treated with sensitive chemicals upon which a latent image can be implanted when they are exposed to light. Although the details of this process need not concern us, a basic understanding is helpful. Modern photographic materials essentially consist of either two or three layers of chemical substances. The bottom layer is merely a carrier or base, consisting of a cellulose-based film, or paper for a print. The top layer consists of the substance in which the image itself will actually be formed. This substance is metallic, normally silver-based, and it also incorporates the dyes needed for colour reproduction. In films (but not in paper prints) there is a third layer, between these two, which is a binding agent linking the base and the image-forming substance. Additional layers, especially in paper used for prints, consist of chemicals which prevent fading, curling and other faults.

When the top layer is exposed to light, a latent image is formed by a process of chemical change. When the film is then developed by being bathed in chemicals, the silver is displaced from the areas which were exposed to light, and the latent image is thus made visible. This visible image is then fixed in a second chemical bath so that it becomes 'permanent', although the extent of the permanence depends upon several factors, including the quality of the chemicals, the water and the film itself, as well as the conditions in which the negative or print is stored. The same essential principles apply to all photographs, whether the material is direct from the camera, or a 'second-generation' copy of the camera film on either film or paper. Finally, prints on paper can deteriorate because the paper itself deteriorates just like other paper.

There have been many varieties of photographic media. Before cellulose bases, or indeed other 'flexible' films, were commonly used, camera negatives were made on many different carriers, including glass and metal. Bases themselves have changed, and older materials still exist in archives. The notorious cellulose nitrate base used for much cine film until the late 1940s, with its dangerous tendency to spontaneous combustion, is still a major problem in film collections. Quite apart from such specific considerations, the chemical base of all photographic materials is susceptible to decay, and images can fade if conditions are not right. Indeed, some images will fade in any conditions, especially those made with the dyes used in early colour films. Some films are more stable than others, and some techniques of processing create a film with better survival properties. Broadly speaking, all photographic materials react badly to continuous and excessive light beyond that needed for the use for which they are designed. All need to be carefully handled, since they can be easily and irreversibly damaged. Such damage may even take place in the viewing or projection device which is needed for all photographic images not reproduced on paper, and the creation of the paper image itself requires the use of equipment through which the negative film has to be passed. Film is far less tolerant of heat, light and dust than is paper, and for the librarian or archivist who seeks to preserve it as part of a permanent research collection, it presents a major headache.

In many of its manifestations, photography is not an archival medium. Only a properly produced and stored monochrome negative film is truly archival; strict standards have been established to determine the requirements for both processing and storage (see pp.119–122). Colour film has a very limited life; loss of colour quality is continuous and rapid almost from the moment when processing is complete.

Recorded sound

Sound recording has a history only slightly shorter than that of photography, although such recordings are perhaps less frequently found in libraries. The most familiar commercial formats – gramophone records, tapes and compact discs – all present preservation problems, but in practice few of them are intended for permanent retention in libraries. Sound archives have their own priorities and concerns, but many libraries do indeed have recorded sound material, and need to know enough about them to optimize their use and storage.

The earliest forms of sound recording, such as wax cylinders, are more often found in museums and sound archives than in libraries; libraries that inherit such objects or acquire them as a part of a collection may well consider redirecting them to a more appropriate repository. The same is probably true of the shellac discs used from the early years of the 20th century until the 1950s. These are very fragile; they will break irreparably if they are dropped or handled carelessly. Vinyl discs, used from the 1950s until the early 1990s, are almost unbreakable, but are vulnerable to damage in almost every other way: damp and heat will cause them to warp; touching the playing surface with a finger will damage it; and the delicate grooves in which the sound is recorded will be ruined by any sort of scratch. Even the stylus (made of sapphire or diamond) by which the disc is 'read' damages these grooves, and causes a comparatively slow, but soon noticeable, deterioration in sound quality. None of these media is truly archival.

Different issues arise with tapes. Open reel, or reel-to-reel, tapes are exceptionally vulnerable to damage because of their design. It is only too easy for tape to work loose from the reel. Cassette tapes are less easy to damage, although they are, like all magnetic media, in danger from external magnetic fields as well as normal hazards such as heat and light. Compact discs, now the most common format of commercial recordings (to the extent that vinyl discs of classical music are no longer manufactured), are more properly considered as electronic media (see p.56).

In practice, recorded sound media are not intended for permanent preservation in the great majority of libraries. They are educational tools or entertainment media, often as part of a loan collection. Librarians can do little more than ensure that they are well-housed, that any playing equipment in the library is of high quality and well-maintained, and that borrowers are exhorted to look after both the objects themselves and their own equipment.

In research collections, where unique material is involved, it is the normal practice to re-record from a master disc or tape, and to make available to users only the copies (or indeed copies of the copies) in order to protect the irreplaceable master. Masters deemed to be of great historical importance are ideally held on tape of the quality used by recording companies and broadcasting organizations for their own archives. Ordinary commercial standard tapes have to be regarded as temporary and disposable, while vinyl records cannot be preserved in perfect condition if they are to be used at all. Compact discs, on the other hand, provided the quality of the data does not deteriorate, are not very vulnerable to physical damage. In one way or another, therefore, recorded sound does not present serious problems except when it is required for truly archival purposes.

Environments for storage and use

An understanding of the physical nature of information storage materials is fundamental to an understanding of preservation. Although, in the last analysis, it is the information itself we normally want to preserve, the format and medium in which we store it is critical, because they essentially determine our ability to retain the content. There will always be some books, documents and other media that we wish to preserve in their original physical form for historical reasons. More pertinently, there is at present no technically and economically acceptable medium into which we can transfer even a significant percentage of our store of written and printed information for permanent preservation. Consequently, the preservation of information still depends upon our ability to preserve the books, manuscripts and other documents in which by far the greater part of mankind's collective memory and wisdom is stored. We know that all of those media are impermanent, but that some are more susceptible to decay than others. We also understand many of the chemical and physical causes of that impermanence, although research continues and results continue to be refined (Havermann 1995). Preservation, therefore, begins with a consideration of how we treat information media in libraries and archives, of how they are stored and used, and, above all, of the environment in which they have to exist.

The preservation surveys of libraries in industrialized countries in the 1970s revealed the extent of deterioration which had taken place even in comparatively dormant materials. Some of this decay was inevitable, since it was intrinsic to the chemical constitution of paper and physical structure of books. It was also clear, however, that both chemical changes in paper and some of the structural problems of books themselves were being exacerbated by unsatisfactory conditions of storage, and by careless or excessive use. Storage conditions are critical to the survival of books and documents, and although counsels of perfection have to be balanced against the realistically attainable, it is necessary to consider the ideal conditions under which materials ought to be kept so that we can assess what is acceptable. However, this must be kept in proper perspective. A book kept in the dark, and preferably in a deep-freeze, would never deteriorate, but it would not be of much use. Preservation is, in the last analysis, simply a means of ensuring that information is available when it is needed, and the preservation of the physical object is only one of several means by which that end might be attained. It follows, therefore, that ideal environments, although they might be justified for that tiny minority of books that are art objects or cultural artefacts, have to be reconciled with the conditions in which both librarians and users can work with the books for the purpose for which they were intended, and also with conditions that are technically and economically feasible.

The environmental enemies of books, with which we are concerned in this chapter, are conventionally classified under five

broad headings:

- temperature
- humidity
- light
- biological infestation
- pollution

As we shall see, this classification is rather crude, but it is a convenient starting-point, and we shall consider each in turn.

Temperature

The problem of temperature can be stated very simply. All organic materials have a 'preferred' temperature at which their useful life is maximized. This is familiar in ordinary life. A piece of wooden furniture in an overheated room, for example, will eventually dry out and crack and perhaps even disintegrate. Similarly, metal objects will expand or contract, however fractionally, in extremes of temperature. Because these phenomena are understood, there are certain precautions that can be taken to ensure that even though unpreventable change will happen, the usefulness of the object will be preserved. Because it is known that the steel used to make railway lines will expand in high temperatures, engineers leave a small 'expansion joint' between successive rails to allow for this. Despite the precaution, in long periods of hot weather rails will sometimes expand beyond the tolerance allowed and will buckle. Greater tolerances are not acceptable, so that occasional faults have to be expected, and appropriate plans devised to deal with them. Railway engineers, however, have no control over the environment in which the rails are placed; they know only the probable climatic variations. The librarian or archivist, on the other hand, is dealing with the comparatively closed and controllable environment of a building.

The tolerance of human beings for temperature variations is fairly limited. The full range of temperatures known to scientists is from absolute zero (-273.15°C) to the alleged temperature at the centre of the sun (in excess of 15 m°C). In practice people can survive only in a minute part of this range, from about -10°C to about +50°C. Human tolerance is slightly increased by the use of special clothing and equipment. Since libraries are for people, the ambient temperature has to be within the small range which their staff and users prefer; there are inevitable slight variations which reflect local expectations of 'normal' conditions.

Modern technology has given us far greater control over the internal environment of a building, to the extent that it can be significantly different from the external climate. We can regulate the air temperature to within one or two degrees, and it can be monitored so that it remains roughly constant even if extreme changes take place outdoors. This capacity is a fairly new phenomenon. As recently as 20 years ago it was not unusual for the interior spaces of buildings to be colder in winter than they were in summer. We have increased the average internal temperature of our buildings by as much as 5°C or even 10°C. We expect all public buildings and enclosed spaces to be heated or cooled for our convenience. Libraries are public buildings, and our expectations apply to them.

If central heating has increased the temperature in buildings in temperate countries, air-conditioning has had the opposite effect in hot climates. Of course, hundreds of millions of people lived in the very hot parts of the globe long before any artificial cooling systems were available, and indeed they still do so where such systems are not in use. Nevertheless, long before Europeans had penetrated to those parts of the world, the inhabitants who had the power and the money designed buildings that were intended to be cool, such as the traditional Arabian houses with open central courtyards and very high, windowless walls. Builders used psychological tricks to give the impression of coolness, such as the fountains and gardens in Moghul or ancient Persian architecture. Occupants employed servants to circulate the air using fans. Europeans followed all of these practices when they settled in the tropics, but the truth is that it is only since the invention of air conditioning that such climates have become truly tolerable to most people accustomed to temperate climates. The massive development of the 'sun belt' states of the south-western United States since 1945 reflects the success of air-conditioning systems in making these hot and inhospitable desert places habitable by people who can afford to create the climate in which they want to live.

The demand for increases in the temperatures in buildings has affected libraries, as it has other places. Indeed, public demand is to some extent reflected in the law, which in some countries, including the United Kingdom, regulates the minimum permitted temperatures for spaces in which employees are required to work. Modern library buildings have central heating systems or air-conditioning systems incorporated into their design, and many older buildings have had such systems installed. The results are generally very pleasant for staff and users. For books they have been catastrophic.

The basic scientific reason for this catastrophe can be stated very simply. The speed of chemical reactions increases with rises in temperature. In general, it approximately doubles with every rise of about 10°C. The rate of increase in the deterioration of paper is even faster, doubling for every increase of approximately 4°C. Deterioration is manifest in two ways. First, the acid in the paper reacts with such catalysts as atmospheric pollutants or the water content in the air; this breaks down the cellulose that bonds together the fibres in the paper. Second, a process of oxidation can take place in certain circumstances, especially with prolonged exposure to light, in which residual metals in the paper will degrade both the lignin and the cellulose, and hence weaken the chemical structure of the paper, perhaps fatally (Priest 1987). These processes of degradation can be inhibited or delayed by controlling other environmental conditions, but high temperatures will always exacerbate the effects of all the inherent chemical problems of paper, even in high quality 'acid-free' or chemically inert paper.

There is no 'ideal' temperature for paper, and for the cheap acidic paper which was used for so many 19th- and early 20th-century books and documents no regulation of temperature can prevent their inevitable eventual self-destruction. However, it is possible to delay deterioration by careful temperature controls, and to do so within limits that are broadly acceptable to both staff and users. One crucial point is that *changes* in temperature are, if anything, more damaging than a consistently high temperature. Thus to move a book from a coolish air-conditioned store to a heated reading room can do more damage than to have the storage area slightly overheated.

In broad terms, paper will tolerate a temperature of about 20–22°C, provided that the air is fairly dry. This is acceptable to people, and attainable in most buildings in which the ambient temperature can be regulated. Ideally, the temperature should be somewhat lower, perhaps as low as 15°C or even a little less. The relevant British Standard suggests that the temperature for the storage of paper and parchment in archives should be in the range 13–18°C (British Standards Institution 1989). In practice, this can be attained only for rarely used materials in storage areas in which there is only an occasional human presence, since such a temperature would now be regarded as being too cold for a working environment. In practice, paper is quite tolerant within these broad limits. For non-paper media, storage temperatures are far more critical. For example, vinyl gramophone records can, in theory, tolerate up to about 50°C, but begin to warp at a considerably lower temperature if they are consistently stored in such heat; about 20°C, with as little variation as possible, is recommended (Heckmann 1987).

Photographic film is the most sensitive medium. The maximum temperature at which celluloid film can be stored for archival purposes is 21°C, and it has very little tolerance of temperature change. More than ±4°C will cause near-fatal problems, so that a constant temperature is more than merely an ideal if the objective is long-term preservation. Processed colour film is particularly sensitive, but in any case is a very unstable medium. Prints can tolerate slightly higher temperatures of up to about 25°C. For long-term storage (for archival master negatives, for example), very low temperature conditions, of below 2°C, are normally recommended (Hendriks 1988: paras. 11.2.3, 11.2.4).

Humidity
Temperature is only one aspect of the ambient environment in a building. The other is humidity – the quantity of water in the air. This is measured as *relative humidity*. Relative humidity (RH) is defined as the weight of the water vapour in a given volume of air expressed as a percentage of the quantity it would hold if it were saturated with water at its present temperature. Thus an RH level of 100% represents complete saturation, while 0% is completely dry (approached only in desert conditions). The natural range of RH in buildings in temperate countries is probably between about 30% and 60%. However, the RH can be modified by mechanical devices. Dehumidifiers remove excess moisture from the air, and can be used on a very small scale (as in a damp room), or on a large scale throughout a building as part of an air-conditioning system.

Where the opposite problem pertains, humidifiers can increase the moisture levels in very dry air. Air-conditioning systems normally incorporate humidity controls, so that in practice humidity and temperature are regulated together. For human beings, perceptions of humidity and temperature are closely associated; there is indeed a scientific link between them. High temperatures and high levels of RH are perhaps the least comfortable climate conditions in which we can find ourselves. Such conditions are common in some equatorial countries, such as Singapore, Thailand, parts of central Africa and large areas of Latin America, and they occur intermittently even in temperate climates such as north-west Europe during the summer. More dramatically, in continental climatic conditions, such as those in the mid-west of the USA, hot and humid conditions in summer alternate with very cold winters. The climate of Chicago, which has precisely these conditions, was famously described as 'nine months of winter and three months of hell'. We also find combinations of high RH and low temperatures; this is the condition loosely called damp by most people. More rarely, we encounter the high temperatures and low RH associated with the Middle East or the American south-west. In order to create a fully controlled environment, an air-conditioning system has to be able to regulate both temperature and humidity to pre-determined levels.

The 'wrong' RH can lead to serious and irreversible damage to paper and other information storage materials. Briefly, if conditions are too dry, paper will become embrittled, while if they are too damp, fungal moulds will develop. Very dry conditions generally exist only in hot desert areas. Fortunately, libraries have been established in such regions only recently, and, like other buildings there, are typically equipped with excellent air-conditioning systems. Provided the system is functioning properly, there is no serious problem of dryness inside the building. It is excessively damp conditions that are both more common and more problematical. The basic physical facts can be stated simply. The moisture in the air will be partially transferred to all absorbent ('hygroscopic') substances with which it is in contact. Paper is hygroscopic, and excessive damp will, in effect, reverse the papermaking process by putting back into the paper some of the water that was removed from it as the pulp was being dried. When paper does become too damp, it attracts the microbiological organisms which manifest themselves as mould. This can migrate from the paper itself through the boards and even into wooden shelves. Moreover, it is a particular problem of hand-made paper, in whose manufacture the drying process was generally less effective than the artificial heat used in Fourdrinier machines.

Damp is a major problem for libraries and archives in many parts of the world, and especially for the great historic research libraries and archival repositories of Europe. Their massive collections on hand-made paper are in serious danger from mould damage if climatic conditions are not properly controlled. In temperate climates, and especially in north-west Europe, dampness is often found in the older buildings in which many major libraries and repositories are still housed. Buildings are inevitably subject to damp after centuries of existence and because some of them are historic monuments as well as working libraries there may even, quite rightly, be legal limits within which any structural alterations or visible modifications have to take place. Many smaller collections, such as those of cathedrals or country houses, are housed in similar buildings, with the added complication that in some cases their owners are unable to bear the considerable costs of whatever environmental improvements might be achieved, even if such improvements were physically possible and aesthetically acceptable. Mould can and does develop in cold and damp conditions, and dehumidification is essential if serious trouble is to be avoided. Once microbiological damage takes place it can rarely be wholly reversed, and almost always leave some permanent trace.

The humidity problem in tropical and subtropical regions is even more dramatic, if only because it is universal. Heat and humidity promote the development of moulds at an uncontrollable rate, and libraries and archives in such places face a major difficulty. This is exacerbated when, as is the case in many developing countries, funds cannot be made available from limited national resources for the installation and very heavy running costs of elaborate air-conditioning systems. In any case, many collections spend decades or even centuries in unsuitable conditions before they ever reach the comparative safety of a public repository. Control can be achieved only by eliminating the worst affected materials, which may at least prevent the further spread of mould, and then by creating a micro-climate in which materials of exceptional importance can be housed. This might mean a special room, or even an airtight cabinet, for these materials.

Mould growth takes place at any temperature in a range of 15–35°C, although it seems to be at its worst at about 30°C. There is a similarly wide range of RH levels at which mould growth will occur in higher temperatures, about 45–60%, although laboratory experiments suggest that, fortunately, development is at its worst only when an exceptionally high 75% of RH is reached. There is a direct and significant relationship between temperature change and the moisture levels in hygroscopic materials. As warm air is cooled, it deposits some of its moisture content, which is absorbed by any hygroscopic materials with which it comes into contact. Thus, cooling the air by 4°C can raise the RH by as much as 10%. In other words, if the temperature is to be controlled by reducing it to levels acceptable to books and users alike, the RH must also be controlled to ensure the books do not absorb the surplus moisture the air extrudes as the temperature falls. Again, this is a particular problem in tropical countries, where RH is naturally about 60% for much of the time, and the temperature an uncomfortable 30°C or more (Wood-Lee 1988: 12–13, 21–2).

It is even more difficult to define an 'ideal' RH than it is to define an 'ideal' temperature. Indeed the two cannot in practice be wholly disentangled. Where a full environmental control system is available, the maximum recommended level of RH for a library is 45–55%, provided the temperature is held at 13–18°C. It is doubtful whether this counsel of perfection can be attained in most libraries, and is in any case barely acceptable to staff or users, but ensuring a constant RH, at a reasonable level, is probably more important than absolute precision in attaining an ideal percentage.

Maintaining an acceptable level of RH is important for paper and parchment, but, as with temperature levels, for photographic materials it is critical. Moulds can develop on photographic film, while the paper on which prints are made is, of course, also subject to the same problems as other paper. For film, the key issue is that a constantly high level of RH will break down the gelatin size used as a divider between the layers of chemical of which film consists. The effect is that the film 'melts'; the image consequently disintegrates long before any mould spores have an opportunity to develop. An RH of 60% is the absolute maximum permissible for film storage and use, even if only short-term preservation is envisaged. For long-term preservation of archival master negatives of research materials, it is almost impossible for the RH to be too low. In practice, a range of 15% to 40% is acceptable for monochrome microfilm, and up to 50% for other monochrome films. For colour films and diazo films, however, the upper limit is substantially lower, being no more than 30%. In fact, for long-term security, storage at near-zero temperature and RH is probably the best method, the ideal combination being perhaps 2C and 2% RH (Hendriks 1984). This, of course, can be attained only for the archival masters, since the internegatives (i.e. negative copies of the master for ordinary use) and positives used for copying and reading or projection have to be maintained at a temperature and RH comparable with that of the studio, reading area or projection room, since sudden change will cause even greater damage.

Light

Humidity and temperature are the two major natural obstacles to the permanent preservation of paper and parchment. An excessive level of light can also cause damage, but it is especially serious, as might be expected, in the case of photographic materials. The damage inflicted on paper by excessive light is chemical. Light, both natural and artificial, contributes to the breakdown of the cellulose structures in the paper. It is also the direct cause of the fading of pigments (such as those used in the illumination and rubrication of manuscripts), of inks and of dyes in colour film and in photographic prints. In addition, of course, direct sunlight raises the air temperature, especially if it passes through glass, and all conventional artificial lighting systems radiate some heat from the light source.

The ideal level of lighting for the storage of library materials of all kinds is total darkness, but only in closed stack areas this can be attained. It is a sensible economy measure, quite apart from being desirable, to ensure that closed-access stacks are lit only when they are in use by book fetchers, except for any legally required minimum level of emergency or safety lighting. Stack lighting, consisting of fluorescent tubes fitted with ultraviolet filters and diffusers, presents no real preservation problems if it is sensibly and economically used. Reading areas are more difficult. Readers need appropriate levels of light for working. For areas in which old or fragile materials are used, fluorescent lighting (which generates comparatively little heat), with ultraviolet filters, is probably the most suitable system, and is certainly the cheapest to operate. If there are windows in reading areas or stacks, it is essential that they too have ultraviolet filters in or on the glass. As in so many other aspects of preservation, we have to be realistic and sensible about this; libraries cannot expect users or staff to work in Stygian gloom. The ultimate objective of preservation is to facilitate, not to inhibit, the use of materials, but to do so in circumstances that are consistent with the continued existence of the materials themselves. Moderate but acceptable levels of filtered light will achieve that.

With photographic materials, we have a different problem. Monochrome film that has been processed to archival standards suffers little from light. Colour film, transparencies and prints, however, are very sensitive. Theoretically, this could be a serious obstacle to preservation, and certainly should be considered in, for example, deciding not to use first-generation colour photographs in a long-term exhibition. In practice, however, photographic materials in libraries and archives are normally stored in total darkness, usually in boxes, albums or folders, which are themselves kept in filing cabinets. Short-term exposure for viewing or projection causes no appreciable damage (Hendriks 1984: para. 11.2.7).

Biological infestation

Because the most common material in a library – paper – is organic, it is subject to biological infestation by mould spores and by insects which are attracted to its chemical constituents as a medium for growth or as food. Mould has already been mentioned in considering the problems arising from excessive humidity. Insect infestation needs to be considered separately. While this problem is at its worst in libraries and archives in tropical countries, it is certainly not unique to them. Indeed, various silverfish, cockroaches and so-called 'bookworms' are comparatively common in temperate countries, especially in older buildings. The various species of insects have slightly different tastes; some prefer paper, while some choose to dine off binding adhesives or even sewing threads. Some particularly fastidious gourmets select a particular kind of paper, such as 'art' paper with a high china clay content in its glazed surface (Parker 1988).

The elimination of insect infestation is an expensive undertaking for which specialists would normally have to be employed. As always in library preservation, prevention is better than having to find − and to fund − a cure. A number of comparatively simple measures can dramatically reduce the likelihood of insect problems. The elimination of vegetable matter from the library and its outer walls is one factor. Planters and flower displays inside, and creepers growing on the outside walls, may be aesthetically pleasing, but they encourage insects. If they cannot be eliminated they have to be monitored. The proper care of all the wooden parts of the library, whether structural or in the form of furniture or shelving, is also critical, since termites breed in wood. It is particularly important in tropical countries to ensure that, as far as possible, the library building is inaccessible not only to termites but also to cockroaches and to the rodents that inevitably abound in such climates. The well-sealed buildings with which we are familiar in temperate regions are neither normal nor indeed climatically necessary in hotter countries, especially where air-conditioning is not an economic possibility. The only option open to the librarian or archivist in such circumstances is to ensure that the books and documents are regularly monitored, and that prompt measures are taken to deal with infestation. If the insects themselves are eliminated, they can cause no damage!

Pollution
The final and most dramatic hazard, and one which exacerbates all the others, is that of pollution. The pollution of the environment

has, of course, become a major political issue in many countries during the last 20 years, and some small steps are being taken to alleviate it. Nevertheless, it is, and will continue to be, a serious danger to both life and property, especially in heavily populated urban areas. Atmospheric pollution has been a consequence of industrialization ever since people first made fires and filled their caves with smoke. It is unavoidable in the modern world, and all we can do is try to contain it at acceptable levels and deal with the consequences of what remains.

Historically, the major pollutant in industrialized countries was in the form of the sulphur products of coal burning. For more than a century coal was the principal fuel for transport, machinery, heating and the generation of gas, electricity and other forms of power. The grime that accumulated on buildings in cities such as London and Paris took decades to remove when coal burning was forbidden or became economically less desirable. The similar patina of grime on books and documents has proved more persistent, even if it is less visible, although a century ago a pioneer of library preservation, William Blades, had already noticed it as a significant enemy of books. Today, coal burning has largely been eliminated from urban areas in the west, although it continues elsewhere in the world, as well as in major facilities such as coal-fired power-stations. Smoke has been replaced as the principal health hazard by carbon monoxide, the major constituent of the exhaust gases of petrol-driven internal combustion engines, and by the other by-products of petrol combustion, especially compounds of lead.

The effects of various pollutants on library and archival materials can be very severe indeed. At the simplest level, dirt is not only unsightly but also damaging; it consists of small particles made up of pollutants. These particles cause physical damage to paper. If the RH is high, the dust or grit may become even more hygroscopic than the paper itself and consequently accelerate the degradation of the cellulose structure. Terms like 'dust' and 'dirt' are, of course, very imprecise. These particles are themselves chemicals which may, for example, contain fragments of acid from combusted fossil fuels or alkaline dust from cement on a building site. Each particular kind of 'dust' may set up its own chemical reaction, although the general effects are the same, and they are all almost equally deleterious. Oxidation can break down cellulose and hence exacerbate the deterioration of paper and parchment. Moreover, not all such chemical pollutants are external to the materials themselves. Some synthetic polymers, which are used in films, magnetic tape, adhesives and indeed in paper, may contain minute quantities of chemical impurities which can lead to internal breakdown of the molecular structure. This is fortunately avoidable; for the use of high-quality film and tape (the media in which the main problems are concentrated) effectively eliminates this particular hazard (Pascoe 1988).

The control of the air quality in a library building is important for people as well as materials. Again, a fully functional air-conditioning system is the ideal solution, since it will filter and purify the air as well as control the temperature and humidity. Where this is not practicable for the whole building, it may be possible to create smaller controlled environments, such as a room or even a cupboard, for materials of exceptional importance or great vulnerability. Security copies of computer tapes, for example, are normally stored in a completely controlled environment. A library may well feel that the master copy of its catalogue deserves this treatment in view of the cost of replacement in case of loss or damage. More traditionally, a book or manuscript of exceptional value might be exhibited to the public only in an environmentally controlled display case. Control of the external environment is ultimately beyond the power of the librarian or archivist, but it is necessary to be aware of it, especially if there are any hazards and sudden changes such as construction work.

Summary

In broad terms, it is not difficult to define the ideal conditions for the storage of library and archival materials. However, those ideal conditions can conflict both with what is attainable and indeed with what is acceptable to those people who use and work with the collections. Neither staff nor users can work properly in cold and dark conditions, and should not be expected to do so. We have to reconcile the ideal with the practicable, and try to achieve an ambient environment in which materials will not suffer more than unavoidable damage. If a building is kept at about 20°C, with an RH of about 40%, little harm will come to most materials while most people will be reasonably comfortable. If the air can also be kept clean, so that neither atmospheric pollution nor infestation by insects or rodents is likely to happen, then the collection will be physically as stable and well protected as a working collection can be. Of course, for some special materials, added protection is desirable. Cultural heritage objects, or historical research materials of great importance, whose physical preservation is deemed to be essential, will have to be protected more stringently. Indeed, they may be made available to users only in surrogate form or under very carefully controlled conditions.

In some cases the information medium itself may dictate the conditions in which it is kept. Colour film and magnetic tape, for example, both require special conditions if their useful life is to be maximized, and the tolerances for these media are far more critical than those for paper or parchment. However, the basic principles of physical conservation are clear enough. A building that is clean, dry and not overheated will not destroy its contents. The design, use and maintenance of the building is therefore an integral part of a preservation programme, for those factors effectively define the immediate environment in which the materials are stored and, in the case of non-circulating collections, used. In the inevitably rare circumstance of a new building being planned, the librarian or archivist will wish to ensure that the basic design is conceived with the preservation of materials in mind. Where funding is available, full environmental controls throughout the building are the ideal, although it has to be remembered that the functioning of the building, the maintenance of its contents and the comfort of its staff and users then become wholly dependent upon the efficient operation of that system. A poor installation, or one which frequently breaks down, is worse than none at all. In countries with unreliable power supplies, for example, or where spare parts or skilled labour for repair work may be in short supply, adaptations of traditional local building designs can sometimes be far better than a western-style building. High ceilings, with or without fans, shaded windows that do not allow direct sunlight to fall on books or readers, and similar traditional practices, are far more effective protectors of the collection than hermetically sealed buildings in which the temperature and humidity will rise almost uncontrollably if the environmental control systems fail.

In the existing buildings in which most libraries are housed, the environment can be controlled to some extent even without a full air conditioning system or anything approaching one. Air pollution, heat and light can all be regulated by simple and comparatively inexpensive means. There is no reason why any library should be dirty; the regular cleaning of books and shelves is a basic procedure in any preservation programme. Windows can be shaded, and, where necessary, screened against flying insects when they are open. Both the level and the sources of artificial light can be regulated. Fitting filters to electric lights is cheap and easy; ensuring the level of light is no more than that necessary for comfortable working conditions is economically desirable, quite apart from any other consideration. Heating systems, if properly maintained, can normally be regulated to within about ±3°C, which should be adequate for most normal purposes. Excessive humidity, especially that of cold damp in older buildings, is more of a problem, but dehumidifiers can help on a small scale, even if they cannot cope with a very large damp space. Proper building maintenance really requires the elimination of large damp areas by other means, for the sake of the building itself as well as its contents. In short, the control of the environment is not beyond the capacity of most libraries or record repositories.

We can define the precise scientific parameters within which materials ought to be stored and housed, but in practice these parameters are almost meaningless. Libraries are for use, and even the great research collections want to attract readers. Unless materials are to be made wholly inaccessible – which can be justified in only a very few cases – we have to accept a working compromise between the ideal and the permissible. If that is achieved, little harm will be done and much quiet good will be the result.

Further reading

The standard work on the history of paper and papermaking is Hunter (1947); on the history of durable papers see Clapp (1972). The basic science of deterioration is explored in Barrow (1959); recent work is accessible in Luner (1990). On the history and practice of bookbinding, see Diehl (1946), Middleton (1988) and Walters Art Gallery (1957). On parchment and leather, see Reed (1972), and on parchment see additionally Clarkson (1994). For summaries of current practices in preservation and conservation of leather bindings see Raphael (1993), and generally Merrill-Oldham and Parisi (1990). For non-book media, there are chapters on sound recordings, moving images and photographs, *inter alia*, in Henderson and Henderson (1991). For more detailed studies of photography, see Hendriks (1984), and of recorded sound, see St Laurent (1991). There is a vast literature on environmental issues; Pascoe (1988) is a comprehensive study and Applebaum (1991) a good practical guide.

Chapter 3
THE PRESERVATION OF INFORMATION

Introduction
In Chapter 2, we defined and explored the classic problems of preservation in libraries. The issues raised there essentially arise from the physical and chemical nature of the materials used for information storage. The properties and weaknesses of paper, adhesives, photographic film and mechanical sound recordings, together with the implications of the various formats used – books, photographic prints, gramophone records and so on – have been considered. The implications of all of this for how libraries are used and managed and an investigation of some of the techniques that can be used to eliminate, minimize or circumvent preservation problems will be the subject of later chapters. First, however, we turn to the rather different issues that arise with another, and increasingly important, class of information storage media and systems: those based on electronically stored data in digitized formats. For the terminology used in this and later chapters, see the Note on Terminology, pp.76–77.

The use of computers is now fundamental to the way in which libraries work and to the provision of services to users. An ever-increasing percentage of the world's information store is in digital form, and can be accessed only by computer. This is not normally direct access except on the smallest scale, as when individuals store information in a data file on the hard disk of their personal computers and access that disk. More commonly, a user at one computer (a 'work station') is gaining access to a file held in another computer, the connection being made through a telecommunications network. The retrieval process may take place tens of thousands of miles away from the storage location; to the end-user, however, this is of no significance unless it incurs direct costs for the communications process that would not have been incurred by local access.

There are some parallels, in terms of intellectual activity, between the process of retrieving information from a digital file and reading the words printed on the page of a book, but they are not very helpful to us in the present context. The essential difference, far more important than any limited philosophical similarities, is that a book is a physical object and, for the end-user, electronically retrieved data is not. Users are simply not aware of the *physical* existence of a database, but they cannot fail to be aware (however subconsciously) of the physical existence of a book, a manuscript, a film or a cassette tape. In other words, the *medium* is hidden; only the *information content* is of any interest or importance to the end-user or even to the information service provider or librarian. Any supposed parallel between using a book and retrieving information from a database breaks down completely when we consider the physical objects involved, and the technologies that underlie them. Reading a book requires skills, but no equipment; to access digital information, both are needed.

It is the technological basis of the use of computers that makes them so fundamentally different from the printed or written word in conventional formats. Because a book is essentially independent of the technology used to produce it, its relationship to that technology ceases once the production process is complete. A book written by a 10th-century monk, or one printed by hand in the 15th century, or a book printed on a steam-driven press in the 19th century are all read in the same way as this book, which has been produced using various computer systems ranging from a simple personal computer with a word processing package, through a more complex editing package to a computer 'typesetting' system and a computer-controlled printing machine. For the reader, the technology which produced the book is irrelevant, except in so far as it might have some marginal effect on legibility.

In retrieving digital information, we are, on the contrary, wholly dependent on the availability of appropriate technology, and our own ability to use it. The information and the technology cannot be separated from each other at the point of use. The closeness of the technology, however, has the somewhat perverse effect of distancing the user from the information. The location and physical form of the information is of no interest to the user: all that matters is that it is electronically accessible. The problem of storage, and hence of preservation, of information is thus removed from the point of use, where it has traditionally been located, to the point of supply. A library (or any other organization for that matter) that provides network access to databases it neither owns nor controls, no longer has any need to concern itself about the storage and care of the medium in which the information is stored. The burden of 'preservation' is therefore transferred to the information provider; the nearest (but still unsatisfactory) analogy with the world of the printed book would be the transfer of responsibility for preservation from the librarian to the publisher. The difficulty of developing that analogy in any remotely realistic way for printed books or journals emphasizes the gulf between the two issues, even though both are concerned with ensuring that the information content of documents is available to users.

These considerations underlie the main theme of this chapter: the preservation for access and use of data stored in electronic formats. The approach adopted is fundamentally different from that in Chapter 2, in which traditional paper materials, with a few late 19th- and early 20th-century additions such as recorded sound and photography, were being discussed. In considering electronic formats, we have to look at issues of technology and access, as well as preservation in the normally understood sense.

Four separate but related topics will be considered in turn:

- the origins and storage of digital information
- the selection of digital information for preservation
- methods for storage of, and access to, archival data
- digitization as a preservation tool.

The origins and storage of digital information

Data is converted into digital form as it is entered into a computer storage system. The systems in current use are:

- keyboarding
- scanning
- handwriting
- voice recognition.

Keyboarding is by far the most usual of these, and is now an almost univeral skill ; indeed it is, for all practical purposes, impossible to use a computer without at least minimal keyboarding abilities. The keyboard layout itself is very much the same as that devised for typewriters in the late 19th century.

At present, the only common alternative to keyboarding is the use of scanning, a system in which a device converts a visual image into a digitized form which the computer can store and process. In its simplest form, the electronic document thus created is a *bit map*, a digital reproduction of the visual appearance of the original. That visual appearance can be reproduced on the screen or as a print-out, but can be manipulated only in a very limited way. In the more sophisticated and increasingly common systems, the scanned data is converted into a fully digitized file which can then be stored and processed as if it had been entered by conventional keyboarding. The source of data for scanning is usually a printed or typed version of the text, or a visual image such as a photograph or a painting, but it can be anything that the scanner can 'read'; most importantly, for our purposes, this includes microfilm. Scanning has not, and probably will not, replace keyboarding as the normal means of input, but it has obvious uses when a digital surrogate is being created (see pp. 122–123) or when the database consists of visual images (Besser and Trant 1995).

There are devices which can 'read' handwriting and digitize it, although it could be argued that there is little conceptual difference between these devices and those which can digitize non-textual images such as photographs. The only serious exploitation of this developing technology is in the form of electronic notebooks and diaries; the user writes on a soft screen with a stylus, and the device converts the handwritten symbols into their digital equivalent. It is likely that such devices will become more common.

Finally, there is the long-awaited goal of computers that recognize the human voice and can convert its sounds into digital symbols for storage and processing. Voice-recognition computers do exist, and it can be expected that they will become more common, and eventually, perhaps as early as the first quarter of the 21st century, begin to displace keyboards as the normal means of data entry. Voice-recogniton is really no more than a form of control system for the computer. The ability to digitize sound, however, is basic to one of the most familiar commercial manifestations of digital technology – the CD or audio tape of recorded speech or music.

All these input devices lead to the creation of files consisting of bytes, which are electro-magnetic imprints. The only significance of this for preservation purposes is that such a record is vulnerable to damage from extraneous magnetic fields, or, in certain circumstances, to variations in the voltage of the electrical power. The physical form is of rather greater significance, for as in the preservation of information stored on conventional materials, the loss of the medium entails the loss of its information content. In the early days of computing, the keyboarder created holes punched into cards or on to streams of paper tape, which were then read into the computer by a device which detected the holes and converted each combination into its digital equivalent. Such systems survived until the early 1980s, but have now vanished. Three media are currently in common use:

- magnetic tape
- magnetic disks
- optical discs.

Tape is most familiar in the form of the magnetic tapes used for audio and video recordings. Tape used in early sound recording systems was electro-magnetic; the tape now in use for many audio, video and computing purposes stores data in a digital format as bytes. Identical tape (although to a higher specification) is used for storing large quantities of data, and, in many cases, for the long-term archiving of such data.

Disks are now as familiar as tapes, as floppy disks, which are inserted into computers for data storage or from which programs are loaded, and as the hard disk, which is an integral part of the computer and typically contains its operating system and the software required by the user as well as user-created files. Once created, files can easily be copied between floppy and hard disks and between disk and tape, and vice versa, provided the software and operating systems are themselves compatible. The choice of format for creation, storage and retrieval of files is dictated by a combination of convenience, cost and, perhaps most importantly, storage capacity.

Optical disc technology has already been mentioned; at present, its most familiar manifestation is as a *CD* (compact disc), containing sound, or a *CD-ROM* (compact disc – read only memory) containing some or all of sound, images and text. In that form, it is essentially a retrieval medium rather than a long-term storage medium. Optical discs are created by copying data from magnetic disk or tape; there may be some enhancement of quality (in the case of audio or video discs, for example) or some additional software may be added to facilitate information retrieval (as is normal with databases transferred to CD-ROM).

All of these formats are vulnerable, and all have comparatively short lifespans. Work conducted in the Magnetic Media Stability Program at the National Media Laboratory in the United States suggests that digital tape has an estimated useful life of some 10–20 years when stored and used under optimal conditions (Van Bogart 1995). The US National Bureau of Standards recommends that tape is stored at about 18°C and in a microclimate with an RH of 35–40%. Such lifespans are acceptable for many purposes, such as the storage of administrative or financial records in the business world, but for long-term archival storage, even in the commercial environment, this is not acceptable. In the pharmaceutical and nuclear industries, for example, a life of 100 years for documents is essential (Stilwell 1995). Librarians and archivists have been considering these issues since the 1980s, when it became clear that digital technologics were going to be of increasing importance (Neavill 1984). Such consideration has, however, become more urgent with the exponential growth in the creation, use and significance of electronic data, and the diversification of its sources of origin. Archivists and records managers have seen this as matter of particular concern, but the boundaries between them and libraries are blurring as all information professionals increasingly focus on information stored in formats that are technologically identical, whatever the form of the records contained in them (Hedstrom 1991).

The selection of digital information for preservation

Until about 1990 librarians had little need to concern themselves with the preservation of electronic data, and were only peripherally interested in the preservation of electronic formats. This attitude was reflected in the first edition of this book, in which barely a page was specifically devoted to electronic media (Feather 1991: 30–1). The interest of librarians focused on the means of keeping output media (especially audio CDs and, increasingly, CD-ROMs) in a useable condition for a reasonable length of time. That attitude is now demonstrably changing (Feather, Eden and Matthews 1996: 46–7), and will continue to do so (Battin 1993). Perhaps the most important reason for this change is the growth of electronic publishing in a variety of formats, and the development of the concept of the 'electronic library'.

The products of electronic publishing can be obtained in the conventional ways, by purchase or subscription. CD-ROMs are familiar in almost all libraries, and are perhaps the most common form of electronic publishing product to librarians and users alike. When properly handled and stored they have an acceptable lifespan, and, in any case, are often reissued annually in a revised version. The most common form of CD-ROM is typically a time-stamped (Graham 1995b: 45–7) version of a database (often, but not invariably, bibliographical) which is owned and updated by the publisher. The librarian's concerns are limited and localized.

Of broader significance, however, are the issues that arise when we consider a database, a structured information file (such as a reference work or a scientific paper) which is indeed analagous to a traditonal information product such as a book or a journal. Its ownership (by the publisher) is not in doubt; the issue that needs to be addressed is the long-term responsibility of the publisher for its maintenance and enhancement. Publishers, however, operate in a commercial world, and one which is increasingly competitive and profit-driven. They cannot be expected to have the sense of archival responsibility, which librarians have traditionally understood to be one of the foundations of their own professional practice. In the age when print media were either unchallenged or predominant, the roles of the publisher and the librarian were quite distinct: the publisher sold the product to the librarian, and the librarian took appropriate steps to ensure its availability and preservation. With electronic media, a new paradigm applies: availability and preservation depend upon the publisher's ability to maintain the database in an accessible form, since the consultation medium (typically CD-ROM) is both impermanent and, in many cases, merely a representation of the state of the database at a particular point in time.

These issues are now beginning to be addressed, most recently and in great detail by a group of leading American academics, librarians and computer scientists (Commission on Preservation and Access 1995). The concept of the 'digital research library' is evolving (Graham 1995a). The function of such a library will be to ensure that scholarly work, or digital primary data of long-term importance, is preserved for the benefit of future generations of scholars and is accessible to them. The concept is a bold one, but there are many obstacles to its realization, two being of particular relevance for our purposes:

- the institutional structure of the digital research library
- the selection of material to form its content

The institutional structure of the digital research library will be unfamiliar. Indeed, it seems highly unlikely to be a single institution, or even to be an institution at all. It is more likely to be a virtual library in its own right, a network established and maintained by a group of information providers and owners for the common benefit of their users and customers. The participants in such networks will not only be academic institutions such as conventional libraries, but also the commercial owners of databases, the publishers of electronic information products such as electronic journals, national governments, international bodies and non-governmental organizations, and a wholly unpredictable number of private, public and semi-private generators and owners of electronic information sources. Each of these groups – and many sub-groups and individual organizations or even particular persons within them – has its own priorities, objectives and constraints, quite apart from the broader legal and social constraints embodied in laws relating to data protection, intellectual property and trans-border dataflow. The diversity of the origin of digital information, and the consequent diversity of ownership of that data, is actually the key to understanding and addressing the issue of its long-term preservation and availability.

The selection of material to form this library from the uncontrolled and ever-increasing mass of information available in electronic formats is perhaps the most important professional issue that is raised by the concept. How are we to select that which deserves long-term preservation? Because it is likely to be in long-term demand, or it is of sufficient long-term significance to justify preserving it against possible demand? Here, at least, some established principles can be applied, by posing some questions – or variations of some questions – that have long been familiar to librarians and archivists:

- is the information of legal or administrative significance?
- is the information of permanent historical, literary or scholarly significance?
- is the information updated in a way which makes earlier versions of lesser or no long-term importance?
- is the information more easily accessible in electronic format than in any possible alternative?

Each of these needs to be considered in turn. A means of doing so is suggested in Table 3.1, in which a number of possible scenarios are explored.

Table 3.1 *Preservation options: electronic data*

	Legal or administrative significance	Scholarly importance	Regularly updated	Suitable format	Action
1	Y	Y	N	Y	Preserve
2	Y	Y or ?	Y	N	Preserve in a better format
3	Y	Y, N or?	Y or N	Y	Preserve
4	N	Y	N	N	Preserve in a better format
5	N	Y	N	Y	Preserve
6	N	N	Y	Y or N	Maintain current file

Legal and administrative requirements may effectively dictate the decision to preserve the data, as we have already suggested (Table 3.1, row 1). The only decision then required is about the suitability of the electronic format, and, if necesary, the selection of an alternative (Table 3.1, row 2). If the desire to preserve the data is driven by scholarly considerations alone, then this level of decision making is driven by the permanence of the present version of the data and the suitability of the current format (Table 3.1, row 3). If the present version is considered to be final and complete, then the best format for preservation has to be selected (Table 3.1, rows 4, 5). If it is not, then the current version must be maintained until an updated version is available, a consideration which equally applies where long-term preservation of any version is considered a desirable objective (Table 3.1, row 6). This typology helps to define, and begins to help us to answer, some key questions about the selection of electronic data for preservation. It also, however, gives a somewhat sharper focus to some other issues. An example will illustrate the point: where the data is regularly updated, the proposed action is the same whether or not the data is considered to be of long-term significance.

If we take the case of a bibliography on CD-ROM, of which a new version is issued annually (an increasingly common electronic publishing phenomenon), an institution need only take steps to ensure that the current CD is available and in useable condition for a year from the time of acquisition. This does not mean that the data itself is of no long-term significance, merely that the publisher has taken the responsibility for its long-term availability. By contrast, a data owner may consider that there is no point in the continuous preservation of the contents of a database of which the previous version is less significant than the current version, or a subsequent version more significant than the current version. This would be case with a library catalogue, where the only version of interest is the most complete – that is, the current version. The same would be true of the records of a bank account; as with the library catalogue, records are not deleted, but a version that does not contain all the records is of lesser interest than one which is comprehensive.

Even these comparatively simple examples illustrate the complex relationship between data owners (or publishers) and providers of information to users (or librarians). In the first case in the previous paragraph, for example, the publisher's answer to our questions would be fundamentally different from the librarian's. In order to generate the information product the librarian wants, the publisher must treat the database as being of long-term significance, analogously with legal or administrative records. Steps therefore have to be taken to ensure its long-term survival, so that it can be updated and used to provide the desired output.

In the previous paragraphs we have implicitly been concerned with what might be called the formal products of electronic data storage and publishing, such products as electronic journals or bibliographic databases. These, however, are by no means the only forms of digital data, and by no means the most complex to consider in terms of preservation management. In a sense, precisely because these formal files and databases are clearly analogous to traditional printed products, we can apply at least some of the traditional criteria, such as quality and long-term 'value'. We have to confront more complex and less familiar issues when we consider manifestations of digital data stores that are either genuine products of a network environment, or results from the creation of a database designed to achieve some particular purpose.

The network environment is generating data at an unprecedented rate: some of this is essentially private, such as electronic mail; some of it is semi-public, such as the contents of e-mail discussion groups; some is clearly in the public domain, and to that extent 'published', such as the contents of sites on the World Wide Web. Among all of this uncontrolled mass of data swirling around in the much-remarked anarchy of the Internet is some material which may be of more than ephemeral interest.

Let us consider first the example of e-mail, now widely used for both business and personal correspondence, displacing not only the written letter and the fax, but also, to some extent, the telephone call. There will, undoubtedly, be e-mail messages that could be of interest to future historians or literary scholars, just as they are interested in the letters, diaries and papers lovingly preserved in traditional libraries and archives. Unless, however, the data is archived electronically, or printed versions of messages are stored in conventional files by their senders or recipients, no record of them will exist. This is perhaps a sustainable loss; in any case, it is one about which we can do nothing. The situation will be no worse for the biographer of a networked late 20th-century subject than it already is for the scholar seeking to write about people of the mid-century who used the telephone, when their parents or grandparents would have written a letter.

Perhaps of rather greater significance, although comparatively small in quantity, is the electronic existence of creative works, whether of art or of literature. Computer art is beyond the scope of our present concerns, but the electronic equivalent of authors' drafts certainly is not. The libraries of the world are repositories of many thousands of literary manuscripts, some of great cultural and literary significance. Indeed, an almost iconic status seems to have been assigned to them. Even those which fall short of being cultural icons (or avoid the pitfalls of that status!) can be very important. Manuscripts of some of the works of most of the major British and American writers of the last two hundred years exist to a greater or lesser extent, and are duly cherished. Many show the process of correction and revision by which the original concept was transformed into the final version of the words of a work of art. A whole academic industry of editing and exegesis has been built upon the foundation of these documents. What is to become of the practitioners of such arts in the future, when the evolution of the author's final creation is devoured by the word-processing software used to generate the text, as each new version overwrites its own predecessor? We may not weep for textual critics, but we must recognize that the electronic age will, in this respect, bequeath to the future a cultural heritage less rich in its variety.

In terms of scale, however, the potential loss of the literary archives of writers of the 1990s and future decades fades into insignificance beside the problems presented by all the semi-formal material created in and through the networked environment of cyberspace. As any user of the Internet knows, there is available, once the tools of finding it have been mastered, an unparalleled quantity of information on almost any conceivable topic. A single example will suffice, from the 'Conservation DistList' hosted at Stanford University (consdist@lindy.stanford.edu) on 25 January 1996 (Figure 3.1). There is a vast amount of information here, from a single day in the existence of one list, in a comparatively esoteric subject. Some of the topics are ephemeral, some are parochial, and some are both; but others are of general interest, and would be difficult to track down in the more formal or conventional literature. The archived version of this list (and thousands of others), accessible through the search engines that have made the Internet such a revolutionary tool for information seekers and providers, has some permanent value. That value can be judged only by the end-user, for there is no quality control on the input into such lists; but the fact remains that the loss of all of this would be a genuine and undesirable loss. How can we, in the long term, ensure access to such material? The problem has usually been seen as one of information retrieval. It is just as acutely a problem in information preservation.

The World Wide Web, the electronic mushroom of the mid-1990s, presents us with comparable issues. Much of the Web consists of straightforward advertising: university prospectuses, publishers' catalogues, electronic shopping facilities, cinema and theatre programmes and reviews, employment agencies and so on. There are some electronic newspapers and a rapid growth in pages gener-

postgraduate conservation courses (mainly for museum curators and art historians

removing lacquer from a 12th century stained-glass window

the effects of the US federal budget on funding agencies supporting conservation activities

patents in conservation products and chemicals

water damage to floppy disks

notes on preservation issues on the California State Library WWW home page

damage from offsetting of ink in early printed books

preservation of bones (from an archaeology student)

meeting of the Society for the Preservation of Natural History Collections

treating deteriorated leather

the practice of rounding and backing in library binding

the preservation of leather gaiters from a World War I uniform

the use of 'gold' inks in a picture printed in California in the 1850s

preserving baleen [whalebone]

preserving the product of a laser printer

the use of book repair tape

removing stains from historic wooden floors

the use of magnetic security strips on CD-ROMs in libraries

Figure 3.1 *A day in the life of a discussion list*

ated by research groups and others who seek to disseminate information as well as to promote a product or a service. All of this is regulated only by the information provider; there is no independent editor as there is for a scholarly journal or in a publishing house. The quality control function is entirely the responsibility of the provider, and the evaluation of how well (if at all) that function has been exercized has to be undertaken by the end-user. Again, however, Websites contain valuable information, some of which may deserve permanent preservation. Who is to select such pages, and who is to be responsible for preserving, and providing access, to them?

It is comparatively easy to formulate these questions, but far less easy to develop satisfactory answers to them. What is clear, however, is that we do need to address the issues of intellectual and electronic integrity of the data archives being created from a multitude of sources throughout the Internet (Lynch 1994). In the last analysis, it will be the information providers who will decide what can and cannot be preserved and made available. The losses to the common store of knowledge will be quantitatively massive, and among the mass will be some that deserved to survive. As this comes to be recognized (and it is information professionals who will have to drive their users to understand the issues), the permanent information in this transitory medium will have to be transferred to other kinds of data archives if it is to survive at all.

We now turn to a final category of product that needs consideration: files created for a particular purpose for which it is possible to envisage different uses in the future. Such datasets have existed for centuries. The use which historians now make of Domesday Book, or of 19th-century parliamentary enquiries, is quite different from the immediate use envisaged by their creators. It is because we can never precisely predict what will be interesting in the future that we must recognize the need to be sensitive and objective in the selection of material for preservation, whatever its material form. The modern equivalents of Domesday Book need to be approached in a similar way. Data archives, supported by universities or other public or semi-public bodies, have become repositories for information thta has been assembled in the course of various activities and is considered to be of more than merely current interest. The most familiar example in the UK is the Economic and Social Research Council (ESRC) Data Archive held at the University of Essex. It consists essentially of data collected in the course of research projects funded by the Council, as well as a wide range of other sources, including various government statistical services. In effect, it represents a form of research output, analogous to the reports, papers and monographs that projects generate. A History Data Unit was established by ESRC and others in 1995 with a similar brief in that field (Lievesley 1996). These public data archive services are the electronic equivalent of a record office, and they are of a comparable importance for historians of the future and social scientists of today (Eaton 1993).

Archives of statistical data, whether gathered by researchers or by government, form one large and important category of data archive, but we should also note another field in which such archives are of increasing importance: literary and other texts. In the UK, the Oxford Text Archive is the longest-established and best-known example. Held on computers at Oxford University, and tracing its origins to the early days of computerized concordance construction (of the text of Shakespeare), it has gradually grown to include a wide range of literary and other texts to which it also provides powerful access and search tools. Similar archives are being developed elsewhere, most notably at the Center for Electronic Texts in the Humanities at the Rutgers and Princeton universities in the USA. The field of text archives is further complicated by the involvement of commercial publishers in the creation of databases of major importance. Perhaps the best known at present are those produced by the British publisher, Chadwyck-Healey, most notably the *English poetry full-text database*, published on CD-ROM, which contains 165,000 poems by 1250 writers, drawn from 4500 printed sources. No library contains all of these sources. The database is therefore a major scholarly tool in its own right as a virtual library of English poetry, without even considering the sort of access it permits to the texts it includes. What is the long-term future of such an enterprise? The CD-ROM versions will not last for ever; it is illegal to copy them: the solution can only lie with the willingness of the publisher, through licensing arrangements or otherwise, to provide for the long-term survival of the database itself (Graham 1995:4; Hockey 1994).

The selection of digital data for preservation is complex and uncertain. The field is one of rapid technological change, in which professional principles are not yet fully developed. There are, of course, some parallels with the issues involved in the preservation of traditional and conventional library and archival materials, but these parallels cannot be pressed too far. Our ability to preserve digital data depends on too many factors beyond the control of the library and archive professions, let alone individual librarians and archivists. With conventional materials we can, in most cases, preserve the information by preserving the information carrier. The carrier – book, document, photograph – is the property of the library, and the issue of ownership of the copyright of its contents therefore does not arise. The mere fact of preserving the object preserves the information, without any copying or improper use.

This can never be true of digital data. A library will, of course, wish to ensure that its property, such as a CD-ROM, is properly used and kept in useable condition, but the librarian has little or no control over the long-term survival of the information content. With rare exceptions, electronic stores are inherently unstable, created precisely because they can be revised and updated at will, so that the current version is always the 'best'. We may eventually decide that we wish to preserve specimens of electronic records selected at particular times and dates; but only the owner of the intellectual property rights can actually implement such a decision. Moreover, the intellectual property rights in much of this data belongs to the private sector, not to governments or public institutions. These owners are publishers, vastly more powerful than the publishers of books and journals ever were. Because they alone control access and enhancement, it is they alone who can ensure preservation for the future.

Storage and access

The storage of digital data is an issue that cannot be separated from the question of access to it, since long-term storage is a benefit to information users only if access is possible. Again, there are theoretical parallels with the preservation of conventional formats, and the provision of access to them, but they are not very helpful beyond the level of fundamental concepts. For both legal and technological reasons, a database can be stored only with the consent and active participation of the owner of the intellectual property it contains. Whether the chosen technique of preservation involves format conversion or refreshment (see p.9), and it will normally be the latter, only the copyright owner can pursue it, and the sheer quantity of storage capacity will inevitably mean that replication of the file (except for normal computer security purposes) is not a practical economic proposition even if permission is given for it to be done.

In the case of files created in the public sector, or as a public good, this is indeed an economic rather than a legal problem. The text and data archives now being created in universities and by scholarly agencies such as the research councils in the UK are intended for permanent preservation, and can be preserved by refreshment, for so long as computers are available with sufficient storage capacity. More problematic, however, are files created commercially, but with a long-term scholarly value. This is, of course, the familiar model of scholarly publishing by commercial publishers, but with a critical difference: once a book is published, and the publisher has made a profit from it, the responsibility for its preservation passes from the publisher to the purchaser. It is the libraries that then take on this responsibility. With electronic databases this is not possible. As we have seen, even if the library acquires the material in the form of a CD-ROM, it cannot permanently preserve it in that format.

This raises a major question to which there is no easy answer and, as yet, no real answer at all. Will publishers of works in electronic formats be willing to undertake the long-term preservation of files? In the case of works that are genuinely completed at the time of 'publication', it is difficult to see a commercial logic in such a course of action. Once the master CD has been created a virtually unlimited number of copies can be made from it for as long as the market exists. For security reasons, it makes sense to keep the database itself during that time in case the master CD should suffer damage, but subsequently there is no commercial reason to do so. The problem arises when the scholarly value of the database seems likely to outlast its value as a commercial product, and the useful life of the medium (such as CD-ROM) in which it was sold. Publishers cannot be forced either to put their material into public domain (except of course by the expiry of the period of copyright, now 70 years in the European Union), or to maintain, at their own expense, databases that occupy expensive storage capacity but have no commercial value. Such databases will, eventually, have to be transferred to data archives, analogous to legal deposit libraries, where they can be maintained and refreshed for as long as they are felt to be worthy of survival. This will almost certainly require legislation, perhaps along the lines recently suggested by the report of a joint Task Force established in the United States by the Commission on Preservation and Access and the Research Libraries Group (CPA/RLG) (Commission on Preservation and Access 1995). The essence of their proposal is that intellectual property owners should be legally obliged to make copies of selected databases available to data archives, under conditions that protect the commercial interests of the owners by ensuring that they control conditions of access during the normal term of such rights (Commission on Preservation and Access 1995: 23–4). At present, American law effectively permits libraries to make a copy of a work for preservation purposes to replace a damaged or lost original, and on the same basis allows backup copies of software to be made (Jensen 1993). It is not clear, however, whether this extends to the substantive information contents of databases, and in many other countries the law is not so generous. Legal deposit of non-print materials is a live issue in Britain, and a matter of growing concern in both the professional and the scholarly communities; a rapid resolution is needed before the losses become unsustainably great (Kenny 1996; Legal deposit 1996).

In the case of 'completed' databases, we can at least articulate the issues without too much difficulty, however problematic the proposed solutions may be. Far more difficult are the more typical files that are continually evolving in the comparatively unstable environment of networked information systems. Even the most formal structured databases are inherently unstable in this context, because it is their nature that they are continually enhanced, refined, augmented and otherwise revised. It is clearly impossible to envisage anything other than token preservation of a sample state of such a database. The selection of a 'date-stamped' example of a database at a particular stage in its existence may be of some significance for future scholars, but this is a decision that cannot be taken at institutional level. Again, some legislation is required to protect both the long-term interests of the academic world and the commercial interests of the database producers and hosts. Although analogues with collection management in conventional libraries have been proposed (Ackerman and Fielding 1995), they are not wholly convincing. The model suggested in Table 3.1 offers one approach to the *selection* of databases; once that or some alternative has been applied, there is a need for a new conceptual framework within which the desired levels of preservation can be attained. This framework can only be national (or, better, international) and will require both legislation and, ultimately, international conventions.

The technical problems of storage are comparatively trivial compared with the legal and economic problems of long-term preservation of electronic data. They cannot, of course, be wholly ignored, but we have to recognise that this is a field in which change is rapid and will continue to be so. The basic problem is that we need to be able to read the data we have stored. Fortunately, we no longer need to think in terms of a continuing relationship between any given file and the hardware and software used to create it. Data can be transferred (or 'migrated') from one format, computer or network to another; indeed this is central to the refreshment process. We do not need to create museums of out-of-date computers that cannot be properly maintained. We merely need to ensure that data formats are sufficiently flexible to enable their adaptation to the protocols and architecture of the electronic environment in which they are to be consulted. It is compatibility of data with its environment that will ensure that preserved electronic data can be accessed.

The basic principles which have been suggested here can be summarized thus:

- preserve information not formats
- preservation requires cooperation between database creators and the institutions that will preserve and provide access
- ensure compatibility of data formats with successive generations of hardware and software.

These principles are sufficiently generalized and flexible to be applied to much more difficult cases than those given as examples.

Consciously created data files, databases and data archives are obvious candidates for consideration for long-term preservation. Much less obvious is the mass of less formal files being created daily through electronic mail, discussion groups and the World Wide Web. It has already been suggested that the principles embodied in Table 3.1 can be applied to such files (see pp.59–61), but the problems of ownership, location and access are vastly more complex than with commercial files. In the latter case, the issues arise out of the very clarity of the legal position about the ownership of intellectual property. In the case of the less formal creations which increasingly characterize the electronic environment, there is considerable room for doubt. In principle, the rights belong to the creator, and in the case of Web pages, for example, that is unambiguous. Far more complex, and yet to be tested in the courts, is whether a contributor to a discussion group is putting information into the public domain (in the legal sense) by making it public on the network. The very informality of the Internet, and its unique development process, has left little time or need for the formulation of such questions. At the present time we can say little more than that the managers of sites and lists have to consider whether any long-term responsibilities might rest upon them. Only when we firmly address the question of creating national or international electronic archives analogous to legal deposit libraries can we begin to consider *how* and *where* such files might be preserved if their preservation were deemed desirable.

Preservation of information is, as was suggested at the beginning of this section, only one of the two related issues, preservation and access. It is, however, the more difficult, for access can be comparatively easily envisaged and achieved. Provided that the conditions suggested here have been met, network access allows access to its preserved digital information. There may, of course, be economic implications for the end-user; communications costs, and perhaps charges for access time itself, will have to be met, and the user will need to be able to make use of the necessary infrastructure of networks, software and hardware. All of this, however, is well understood and administratively familiar, for it is the essence of the network environment itself. Access ultimately depends primarily on the preservation of the data in a format compatible with the network, and at a location that can be reached through the network.

Digitization as a preservation tool

We now turn to a final issue, which has been the subject of much professional interest in recent years: the use of digitization as a tool for the preservation of information originally created in conventional formats.

Digitization has been widely canvassed as one solution to the problem of information preservation in libraries and archives. It has, in theory, much to recommend it. Format conversion is perhaps the only feasible solution to some preservation problems; some of these, such as newspapers, have already been identified. Conversion to a digital format gives the user a whole range of new search tools, since what is created is a file that can be manipulated just like any other electronic data file. It is, therefore, possible to conduct searches of an extent and complexity that would be impossible in a long run of a newspaper, or to conduct linguistic analyses which would similarly be all but impracticable if undertaken by any other method. The problem is, of course, that the files created by digitization are subject to all the same problems as files created by any other means for any other purpose. If digitization is indeed a means of preserving information originally published in other formats, it must be justified both technologically and economically, given that the file itself can be preserved only by a commitment to refreshment at appropriate intervals. This factor alone has acted as a partial deterrent to some would-be exploiters of the method (Gartner 1993); although the fears are perhaps now being overcome, major cost issues remain (Conway 1994).

Despite this, however, there have been some important projects in this field, to the extent that digitization is now a working tool for the preservation of information. In the UK, the British Library has supported a number of important advances. A demonstrator project was developed which effectively showed technologies that could generate an acceptable product (Barden 1994; Broadhurst 1993; Shiel and Broadhurst 1994); nevertheless, even the investigators themselves were cautious in their conclusions, and argued that many problems remained before a fully operational programme could be instituted (Barden 1994: 215). The British Library has also commissioned a major study of the preservation of digital material, which explores many technical issues (Hendley 1996). Perhaps the most spectacular product of the British Library's involvement to date has been the digital version of the unique late tenth-century manuscript of the Anglo-Saxon poem *Beowulf*, which was damaged by fire in 1731. The electronic images have proved to be acceptable to scholars, and will form the basis of a complex CD-ROM product that will include an electronically enhanced visual version of the text of the manuscript itself, which will be easier to read, important 18th-century transcripts of the damaged original, a translation, a glossary, a textual commentary, references to relevant archaeological material and other editorial matter. The *Electronic Beowulf* perfectly exemplifies the almost unlimited potential of digitization as a tool for the preservation of texts and the furtherance of scholarship (Beowulf rewarded 1995; Kiernan 1995; Prescot 1994).

In the USA, a number of research and development projects have been conducted over several years, the most recent and most important being a collaborative effort between Cornell University and the Xerox Corporation, which reached very similar general conclusions to those of the British Library's investigators (Kenney and Personius 1992). Appropriate technical standards were identified, as were some key professional issues, such as selection of material for preservation (see pp. 57–67), and the need for further research into both the technology and the environment in which it will be used (Kenney 1995b: 4). A key element in the acceptability of these digitized products as a substitute for the original will be the standards applied to their creation and dissemination. Technical standards exist for such matters as file-transfer protocols across networks and the formats and encoding of files themselves, and have been adopted within the digitization community (Besser and Trant 1995: 36). It remains the case, however, that the quality standards for the images – the most immediately critical issue to the end-user – are still a matter of proposal and debate (Mason 1994; Weaver 1994), and the subject of one of the proposed 'support structures' whose development was identified as a desirable future action by the CPA/RLG Task Force (Commission on Preservation and Access 1995: 38). Microfilm has been widely identified as the best intermediary medium for scanning when a high-quality product is essential and the originals are very diverse in format and appearance. This conclusion has been reinforced in one of the largest European digitization projects, in which the Bibliothèque Nationale de France proposes to digitize some 100,000 volumes before 1997 (Maignien 1995). The same procedure has also been followed at Yale (Lynn 1995: 4).

The visual quality and intellectual integrity of the digitized file is only one of the user's concerns; the other is the means of access to the file. This can, of course, be via a network, but a number of the digitization projects are also investigating or producing other media. The Bibliothèque Nationale de France envisages that its digitized books will initially be available on a Local Area Network in the Library, and later by remote access (Maignien 1995). As we have seen, the *Electronic Beowulf* will be published in its fullest form on CD-ROM. The Cornell/Xerox project has experimented very extensively and with some success with microform *output* from the digitized versions (Kenney 1993a; Kenney 1993b: 9-10; Kenney 1994).

The relatively smooth transfer that can now be achieved between conventional and digital formats and media probably points the way to the future. Digitization remains an expensive option. Long-term costs are still necessarily speculative, but despite projected decreases in the real cost of technology, calculations made by the CPA/RLG Task force, based on data and assumptions generated at Yale University Library, suggested that for a substantial digital archive (equivalent to some 200,000 *new* volumes per year) it would be Year 7 before the digital archive showed even a marginal cost benefit over conventional depository storage of the equivalent number of books (Commission on Preservation and Access 1995: 30–4). This factor cannot be ignored by libraries seeking to exploit the possibilities of digitization as a tool of format conversion and information preservation.

Conclusions

There are, at present, more questions than answers. Many of the basic technical issues about the preservation of electronic data and formats are resolved at least in part, but the professional issues which arise are only now being fully articulated and developed. Yet these issues are very real. Huge and important files already exist and are being augmented every day, even as new files come into existence. More and more information is being created in a networked environment, where its only existence will be in the virtuality of digital storage media. Some, but by no means all, of the information in these databases and on the networks is of long-term legal, administrative, cultural or scholarly importance. Principles of selection for preservation are needed as a high priority, and the evolution of both standards and methods for storage, preservation and access is essential. Yet the pace of change in this field is so fast as to be unique in the history of information storage, retrieval and communication. The long-term view is an unfamiliar perspective for most of those most actively engaged at the leading edge of development and application. It is for this reason that the more reflective view taken by the CPA/RLG Task Force is so important, and that the research designed to develop techniques of using digitization as a tool to preserve documents originally created in analog formats is of such great significance.

It has been emphasized throughout this chapter that the solutions to most of the problems discussed are beyond the scope of individual libraries. The networked environment, which increasingly encompasses the work of electronic data and digitization, forces the consideration of the issues into a wider sphere. National libraries, research libraries, professional bodies and the information industry are all playing a part in providing a better basis of understanding for the identification of issues and the solution of problems. They will have to continue to do so if we are to be enabled to preserve an image of the digital present to compare with the images we have inherited – and seek to preserve – from the analog past.

Further reading

The basic text on records management, the activity which underpins much of what is discussed in this chapter, is Penn, Pennix and Coulson (1994). The most recent comprehensive, but accessible, technical study is Hendley (1996). For a rather broader study of the issues, see Commission on Preservation and Access (1995). Finally, for studies of various aspects of the subject, including linkages into other aspects of information work, see Dempsey, Law and Mowat (1995), and Helal and Weiss (1996).

A note on terminology

Much of the subject matter of this chapter represents a comparatively unfamiliar approach both to preservation and to the use of IT in and by libraries and other information agencies. In an attempt to avoid ambiguity, while conforming to generally accepted usages, the following distinctions have been consistently followed:

Digitization is understood to mean the conversion for data into digital form. The original (analog) data may be text or graphics or some combination of the two, electromagnetically recorded sound, photographic images and so on. The essence of the process is that when it is complete, the digital file can be handled as if it had originally been created in that form by keyboarding or scanning.

Electronic is used as the top-level term embracing all aspects of both **digital** and **analog** data that is stored in and must be read through a computer.

Digital data, which is the principal concern of this chapter, is either **computer readable** or **device specific**.

Computer readable data consists of files of bytes and can be read in any computer with which the storage format is compatible, while **device specific data** can be read only on a device designed for a particular format, such as CD-ROM. In this sense, device-specific data is a sub-set of computer readable data.

Further sub divisions of computer readable data are:

- **databases**, in which the information content is structured into records and fields; the archetypal example is the library catalogue.
- **data files**, in which the information is unstructured, and can therefore be stored, searched, retrieved and reformatted for output in many different forms. Examples include word-processing and spreadsheets, and, in the network environment, electronic mail and Websites. The data need not be alphanumeric: it can consist of images or sound, or a combination of images, sound and text. Sound is most familiar as the digital tapes and audio CDs that are now the norm in the recording industry; multimedia disks are becoming equally familiar.
- **software**, which should probably be treated as a separate category since it is portable between databases and data files. It is used to drive the computer and the databases and data files it contains.

All of these can exist in a range of physical formats used as **storage media**, such as **tapes, hard disks, floppy disks**, or **optical discs** (CDs).

For our present purposes, it is the computer-readable databases and data files that are of primary importance. The storage media are a means to an end (the preservation of the information encoded in the digital data) but are not intrinsically subjects for preservation.

Chapter 4
PRESERVATION POLICY AND LIBRARY USE

Introduction

The preservation problem in libraries and archives has a physical origin: the paper, parchment and other materials upon which information has traditionally been stored are subject to deterioration at a rate which is influenced by the environment in which they are kept and used; electronic data is susceptible to physical and electromagnetic damage, and has to be made available through properly functioning networks and hardware. Access to information, and the preservation of media and data which facilitates access, cannot be expected simply to happen; they have to be directed like any other aspect of library activity. A retention, preservation and access policy is needed that will determine priorities and methods, if only to ensure that limited funds are not dissipated on work of little or no value. Policies have to be based on an understanding of principles, but also derive from a knowledge of local circumstances and from a broad concept of the function of the institution.

Within an institution, all of these factors have to be taken into account in evolving a preservation policy. As we have seen, comparatively few British libraries have yet recognized the need for formal policy statements, although probably more now have a preservation policy than the raw data might suggest. While only about 10% of libraries reported that they had a *written* preservation policy in 1993, considerably more than that had *de facto* policies in place to cover such matters as binding, retention and disposal (Feather, Matthews and Eden 1996: 52–4). Few, however, have explicitly recognized the essential continuum of selection, acquisition, storage and use followed by a choice between disposal on the one hand and retention and preservation on the other, and even fewer have fully appreciated the wider dimension of the last stage of this process. Nevertheless, preservation policies do exist, and many libraries which do not have them are seeking to develop them.

The basic objective of a preservation policy is best defined as being to ensure that the materials and information the library's users can reasonably demand will be available when needed. Hence it must be based on an understanding of three related factors, one general and two specific to each institution:

- the use of information and the literature which contains it and the local applicability of these general principles;
- the demands of the library's own clients and its ability and willingness to meet those demands from its own holdings of books and other media;
- the intellectual quality of its existing stock.

These three factors help to define the relationship between stock and users, and the ability of the stock to satisfy need and reasonable demand. A fourth factor, however, relates to the stock as a collection of objects housed in a particular place, for no meaningful preservation policy, however much it deals with questions of access to information from other institutions and sources, can ignore the physical condition of the collection and the buildings in which it is housed. While this is not subordinate to the first three, it does, however, depend upon them, for until the use and quality of the stock is understood, there can be no effective guidelines for interpreting the results of a physical survey, or even for determining which parts of the collection will be the subject of such a survey.

We now turn to a detailed consideration of these factors.

The demands of clients

All libraries have a more or less clear idea of the client groups at which their services are principally aimed. The public library is the most comprehensive, with its avowed intention of serving all the inhabitants of a particular area, and of providing them with everything from leisure reading to high-level information services, as well as acting as a referral point to specialized information agencies, a point of contact with regional, national and international document delivery services, and a point of access to distant information sources. Within a large public library system there are obviously significant variations in the use of particular services and the functions of particular branches, but the provision of a comprehensive service is the overall objective of the system. Other types of library have more limited client groups whose information and literature needs can be more specifically defined and perhaps therefore more easily met. The library of a school, college or university, for example, primarily exists to serve the members, both teachers and students, of the institution. Its services are defined by the needs of these clients, and its holdings largely determined by their interests. This is even more true in a special library, whether private or public, which exists for the sole purpose of serving a very well-defined, and perhaps very small, client group whose needs are very specific. Services may be offered to those outside the parent organization, but they are secondary and often part of mutually beneficial cooperative schemes.

Of course, there is overlap of both use and purpose. Those with access to a university library may well make use of a public library for leisure reading; the employees of organizations with special libraries may have access to a university library for books and information not available to them directly, and so on. Similarly, some university libraries (although comparatively few) see themselves solely as providers of textbooks and current information rather than, to a greater or lesser extent, long-term archival institutions in which at least a part of the holdings is intended for permanent preservation. On the other hand, there are some collections in public libraries which are clearly of permanent interest and importance, and for which long-term preservation is desirable.

This diversity of function and operation among libraries, even within the same sector, means that although we can adduce general principles and suggest ways in which policies can be developed and effectively implemented, it is not possible to prescribe the policies themselves. A policy for preservation, retention and access can be developed only out of a library's analysis and definition of its own role, and is indeed fundamental to the realization of that role. Moreover, within an institution or a system, it is possible (and in larger libraries almost inevitable) that there is actually more than one preservation policy, or rather that the policy differentiaties between various parts of the stock. In both public and academic libraries, distinctions are traditionally drawn between special collections and the general stock. Definitions of 'special' can themselves vary; disposable ephemera in one library may be a legitimate part of a research collection in another. Controlled storage areas, often closed to the general public, and designated areas for consultation, are an almost inevitable concomitant of creating special collections that it is desirable to house and consult under protected conditions for reasons of preservation and security. On the other hand, all libraries also want to maintain a working stock of material to satisfy general and immediate use. Maintaining the physical condition of the loan stock so that it is acceptable to users is a very different matter from ensuring that special materials are treated in a way that ensures their long-term survival, yet both of these sets of activities are integral parts of a preservation policy. That policy is ultimately to be determined by what the library has to do in order to serve its clients, which, in some cases, will mean also serving its clients in the future as well as those of today.

In serving today's clients, a library may legitimately take a decision not to acquire or not to retain. Considerations of both space and money make this essential as well as desirable. For example, the library of a university in which research is a comparatively minor activity may concentrate almost entirely on the provision of student learning materials at undergraduate level. Higher-level materials will be obtained through document delivery services, but to facilitate this the library will own or have access to appropriate bibliographies, indexes and abstracts. This is a pattern that is increasingly common in many British universities, especially those established in the 1990s as instruments of mass higher education. Similarly in public libraries, the limited shelf space can be devoted only to the stock most likely to be in demand by users; more specialized material, or material in lesser demand, may be held in reserve stores either on the premises or (more often) at some central point to which all branches have access. But public libraries also make use of interlending and document delivery services, and special libraries use them heavily. The balance between ownership of materials and providing the means for users to gain access to material (or to its information content) is an increasingly important factor in managing the collection and access policies of all libraries. It has obvious implications for preservation policies, not least in helping to define more precisely the parts of the collection that are indeed intended for longer-term preservation and use.

The quality of the stock

The objective measurement of the intellectual quality of the stock is an essential element in determining a preservation policy. The random preservation of individual items with no context in the collection is a waste of limited resources. Stock assessment has, until recently, been a somewhat subjective exercise, at the level of 'we have always been strong in . . .'. Such statements from long-established members of staff with a deep knowledge of the collection are not to be despised, but they can hardly form the basis of an objective evaluation of the library's holdings. The system known as Conspectus, developed by the members of the RLG in the United States, is one attempt to overcome the problem of excessive subjectivity.

The basic principle of Conspectus is both simple and attractive. The existing collection is assessed using such criteria as language coverage (English only, all western languages, etc.), format (books and journals, books only, all formats, etc.) and intellectual level or scope (textbooks; research monographs, etc.). These are recorded by means of codes on a form that also allows for the use of 'scope notes' to add more sophisticated comments. The Conspectus is divided into subject areas using a standard classification scheme. Thus a library can arrive at an evaluation of its collection which will, for example, indicate that in DDC class 020 it has a collection at Level 4 ('research level'). This, therefore, contains all the major works in the field, including specialized monographs, a comprehensive collection of indexes, bibliographies and abstracts and a wide range of primary and secondary journals. The subject areas are defined, as in this example, by the broad use of a classification system. In the RLG version this was, inevitably, Library of Congress, although Dewey has been used in the UK and elsewhere. For the most part, Conspectus has been applied in academic and research libraries. Indeed, the original concept within RLG was that Conspectus would provide a means of comparing collections and coordinating collection development policies between certain libraries within the group. The format was devised so that the Conspectus could be mounted on the Research Libraries Information Network (RLIN) database, and it was as a tool of collaboration that Conspectus was presented to the profession at large (Stam 1986). However, there is no reason in principle why it should not be used in every kind of library, and for purely internal purposes. In the UK, the British Library undertook a substantial exercise as part of a larger review of its collection development and retention policy (Enright, Hellinga and Leigh 1989: 30). By far the most active British project, however, has been in Scotland, where Conspectus has been used internally by the National Library, and also to give a broader picture of the holdings of Scottish academic libraries and research collections (Matheson 1987).

The potential relevance of Conspectus to preservation lies in its apparently unprecedented power as a tool for collection management. The existing collection can be measured against a library's collecting objectives, which can themselves be defined in the same terms of language, scope and level. A direct, if somewhat crude, comparison is then possible between objectives and achievements. Where the two do not correspond, collection development policies and acquisitions can be adjusted accordingly. In the financial circumstances prevailing in most libraries today, this is likely to mean in practice that there is a more effective mechanism for the management of contraction; even that, however, is better than unregulated and inconsistent individual decisions on withdrawal without replacement, cancellation of subscriptions and so on. It is in this dimension that the information derived from Conspectus, or other qualitative surveys of library holdings, can be used in the development and implementation of a preservation policy.

Once the quality of the collection has been assessed, and the future pattern of development of particular parts of it determined, better decisions can be taken about the preservation of existing stock and future acquisitions. If it is determined that a particular subject area is already at research level, and is to be maintained and developed at that level, then it follows that the bulk, and perhaps all, of the holdings in that field are intended for permanent retention; the exceptions (duplicate copies of textbooks, for example) will be few and minor. If these materials, and older materials already in the library, are to be retained for research purposes, then it follows that more preservation efforts will have to be directed towards them than towards other areas of the collection that have been determined to have a lesser value in that particular library. This approach has been criticized as a 'blunt instrument' (Naylor 1988: 26), and it is certainly not perfect; it has particularly serious limitations in dealing with very specialized collections, or with subjects in which journal literature is more significant than monographs. Even so, there is growing evidence that, when it is used with discretion, Conspectus can be a useful instrument in a collection management programme and can have valuable implications for preservation policy.

The use of information

Preservation is not an antiquarian exercise for keeping objects from the past simply because they are old: it is a managerial tool for making information available to users. The basic issues of preservation policy can therefore best be stated in terms of the intended or predicted use of the materials. We can reduce these issues to three fundamental questions:

• what is to be preserved?
• for how long is it to be preserved?
• by what means is it to be preserved?

The answers to these three questions provide the foundations upon which a preservation policy can be built, but each answer requires an understanding of a wide range of issues about the library as a whole.

What is to be preserved: the issue of selection

It is both impossible and undesirable to preserve everything in its original physical form. Even if it were possible, it would be impracticable for all libraries to do so, because of limitations of space. If the collection is to be properly developed and managed, there must be a process of selection for preservation. From this it follows that some items are effectively being selected for non-preservation, although this can be at several different levels, as we shall see.

How is this selection to take place, and what factors are to be considered? Four basic parameters can be suggested:

- subject
- format
- age
- use

The **subject** of a book is fundamental to the decision to acquire it for a library, and as important to the later decision to retain or dispose of it (Smethurst 1988). Within an individual library, the decision can be taken that a particular field is of such importance to clients that all materials acquired in that field have to be preserved. In due course, this may come to be treated as a 'special collection', and, indeed, in the long term, all material intended for permanent preservation will have to be subjected to 'special' treatment of some kind. It is indeed in the creation and definition of special collections that preservation becomes central to the collection management policy. The decision to preserve materials in the long term (that is, for the foreseeable future) carries with it the responsibility of developing a preservation management and conservation policy that permits their survival. This will often involve special storage, special conditions of access and use, and so on, and will, in some cases, necessitate the creation and maintenance of special catalogues and other finding aids to assist the researcher. In essence, we are seeking to arrive at a balance between the demands of current and future users. Where the material is acquired because its subject is of long-term significance to the library's users, steps will have to be taken to ensure its long-term survival. For example, among British academic libraries, nearly two-thirds hope to retain more than 75% of their stock permanently (Feather, Matthews and Eden 1996: 31–2); their ability to do so will ultimately be determined by their ability to pay the costs involved.

The **format or medium** may in itself define the practicability of preservation. As we have seen, some of the magnetic media cannot be preserved with any guarantee of data integrity for more than a few years, just as items printed on acidic and embrittled paper will eventually disintegrate. A preservation policy defines what materials are to be preserved if possible, and also what categories of information are to be preserved even though that information will be transferred to another medium (from paper to film, for example), or have to be regularly refreshed to ensure its survival. The preservation decisions are thus moving away from purely material considerations into more complex issues relating to the preservation of the information content of the materials. As this factor becomes more weighty, it also brings into play the need to consider and evaluate the availability of the information elsewhere and ease of access to it, particularly if that access is electronic.

The **age** of the material can be a determining factor in several ways. A research library may decide, as a matter of principle, to preserve all books printed before a certain date, even if surrogates are made or acquired to protect the originals from over-use. This is increasingly the case with historic newspaper collections in British libraries. At the other extreme, it may be felt that some categories of material can be disposed of when they reach a predetermined age, because their use in that particular library can be regarded as ended. For example, public libraries do not generally keep runs of all the national newspapers to which they subscribe, often in multiple copies, for daily use. In the majority of cases, however, decisions are not so clear, nor their determination so mechanistic, nor their outcome absolute. Some public libraries would hope to turn over their fiction stock in branches on an annual or biennial basis; some, but by no means all, of the books that had been through a complete cycle would be transferred to reserve stocks against possible future demand. In academic libraries it is good practice (although for financial reasons increasingly difficult) to dispose of existing editions when a new edition of a book is published, unless there is some reason (such as the creation of a long-term special collection) for not doing so. These issues can only be resolved locally; each one, however, carries with it those familiar implications of direct and indirect costs of storage, maintenance and record keeping.

Most important of all, however, and most neglected in this context, is the factor of **use**. Materials that are wanted and used by the library's clients have to be preserved, or acceptable substitutes provided. Other materials may be permitted to survive, but utility has to be the ultimate determinant of preservation. Of course, further definition is needed. Acceptable levels of use can legitimately vary from many times a day to a few times in a century. Crude measures cannot be applied, but where it can be shown that materials are unlikely ever again to be used in a particular library, and there is no other reason (such as age) for preserving them, then it is legitimate to regard them as candidates for disposal. These issues, however, are not simple. The concept of 'benign neglect' – suggesting that materials left undisturbed will be undamaged – is fundamentally flawed, for they will deteriorate, however slowly, whether they are used or not. Moreover, all materials occupy space (with cost implications) and have to be recorded in catalogues and other finding aids. No general rules are, however, possible. Even a low level of scholarly use of material may justify preservation in some form if the collection is important or unique; responsible decisions about retention and disposal of materials can be taken only in a context wider than that of the individual institution, although in practice this will lead to automatic disposal of out-of-date materials in all but a handful of scholarly research libraries. The essential point is that the decision should be based on a clear understanding of *why* an item is to be preserved, and a reasoned judgment of how and why it will be used.

For how long is it to be preserved: the issue of time

The time factor is a neglected aspect of preservation policy. There is an underlying assumption in much of the literature that there is a stark and simple contrast between no preservation at all and permanent retention. Not only is this illogical in theory, it is demonstrably untrue in practice. In practice, the utility of library materials is determined in part by their age, just as it is in part by their subject matter, physical constitution and material condition, and their present and future use. It has already been suggested that yesterday's newspapers are of little interest to a public library. Even this apparently obvious statement needs some qualification. Most public libraries, for example, consider it their duty to preserve a complete run of newspapers published in their own locality. In that respect, they take on the archival function of a research library, and therefore commit themselves to the preservation of information and of materials. Similarly, newspaper cuttings on specific subjects are an important part of the information resource in many special libraries. Such cuttings are assumed to have some value beyond the date of publication of the newspaper. How long will they be kept? And what measures will be needed to ensure that they are usable for the whole of that time?

Specific questions of this kind can be asked about many categories of material. Is it the policy to retain annual reference books when the next year's volume is published? If so, why is this done? What level of use is expected? Will they be held on open access or in closed storage areas? All of these factors will affect preservation decisions. To put the matter at its crudest, if the covers come away from *Who's who* in November, and it will be discarded when the new volume is published in January, what is the point of anything other than simple palliative measures to keep the book in usable condition for a few more weeks? If it is intended to preserve it after that time, it may indeed be necessary to repair it properly, but if it is to be discarded the expenditure cannot be justified.

One particular category of material can be highlighted to permit a further exploration of this dilemma. It is well known that research scientists rely very heavily on journal literature, but that papers are most frequently consulted very soon after publication. Thereafter, consultation is infrequent, and in some disciplines almost unknown. The phenomenon known as citation decay sets in at a fairly early stage in a paper's life. Moreover, although the rate of decay does indeed vary between different branches of science, the principle is universal. Bibliometric studies have shown that the 'half-life' of a scientific paper (i.e., its generally useful lifetime) may be as little as four to five years, after which it is rarely cited (Meadows 1974).

These considerations are fundamental to managing a collection of scientific journals, not least in its physical dimension. If the working life of a journal is five years, for example, is it possible to justify the cost of binding it? Indeed, the process of binding may actually reduce the usefulness of the journal, since it will be out of use for at least a few days, and more often several weeks, while it is being bound. This will typically be some three to twelve months after publication. Yet this is the height of its useful life, when the papers it contains are beginning to be listed in annual indexes and abstracts and the demand for them consequently increases. The supposed conflict between preservation and use barely exists in such cases. Provided a five-year working life can be assured in other ways, binding cannot be justified even in terms of the use of the materials, let alone in economic terms. Other questions arise for such journals. When the half-life of the journal has been reached, is there a case for disposal? Shelf-space is expensive, and long runs of periodicals can occupy far more of it than their use justifies. For most scientific libraries (and certainly, and perhaps more importantly, for most scientists), currency is far more significant than archiving, and the permanent preservation of material that might one day be of historical interest is more properly left to others.

By what means is it to be preserved: the issue of methods

The decision to preserve can be implemented only if a suitable method of preservation is available and if the money and skills can be found to use the chosen method. The range of options available is large. At the one extreme is the restoration, conservation and permanent preservation of the object as nearly as possible to its original form. Such a solution is occasionally adopted for books and documents with historic, almost iconic, status, such as Domesday Book or the Book of Kells. Ironically, one consequence of this course of action is that the original document is then treated as a museum object, and consultation is normally through some surrogate medium. Indeed, in both these cases, there are far better means of accessing the text of both these books than by consulting the original, and even the visual appearance of the original can, for the vast majority of people, be adequately represented by good facsimiles.

A more common case, familiar in many libraries, is that of literary first editions. It is, of course, perfectly proper for research libraries to preserve these as important evidence for the history of the text and the publishing history of the book. A Dickens novel in its original parts, or a copy of the first edition of *The waste land* are historical evidence in their own right, as well as being of textual significance. The great majority of users, however, need not consult the first edition; they want a readable and accurate text. In fact, in the case of many authors (and not only those of earlier centuries than our own) an accurate text, representing the author's final version, may be found only in a scholarly reconstruction based on several printed editions and perhaps on surviving manuscript versions, corrected proof sheets, and so on. In other words, the 'first edition', although bibliophilically interesting (and perhaps of considerable commercial value) is not necessarily the best means of meeting the needs of the library user. If such books are to be preserved, they have to be identified as part of a special collection and given appropriate treatment. That may include expensive conservation work, especially if, before acquiring this iconic status, the book was in regular use as part of the general collection, a common fate of both fiction and poetry, which tend to acquire their classic or literary status only some years after publication.

Within a collection, when the decision to retain the original has been taken, a number of techniques can be adopted to preserve it against further damage. Physical intervention can mean anything from full-scale conservation treatment to minor repairs. What is needed is to reconcile the physical condition of the book with the conditions under which it can be stored and used. Ironically, books that are well-protected in special collections may actually need less conservation work than those which are expected to survive the hazards of general use and circulation. In special collections, expedients such as portfolios, boxes and slip cases are commonly used to prevent further damage once it has been established that the book has no 'active' problems such as mould or infestation. Such measures are cheap, simple and effective. We shall return to this matter, and to the various options available for rebinding and the repairs of existing bindings in Chapter 6 (see pp. 128–138).

Where the format is of little interest, or perhaps cannot be effectively preserved in a useable condition, the question of substitution has to be addressed. This may take the form of simply buying another copy to replace one damaged beyond use. For financial reasons this practice is perhaps less common than it was, but is still to be found. Perhaps this is most often the case when a book is replaced by a subsequent edition. Substitution of one book by a copy of the same book is a means of making the information content available to users. Where this simple approach cannot be adopted, however, and it is still desirable to preserve information content, more complex solutions must be sought. The use of surrogate media is the normal approach here. A microfilm (or perhaps digital) version of the work will offer the information content (and a facsimile of its appearance) to the user. It may even offer more than that, in terms of indexing and search facilities, and perhaps a complete run of a newspaper or periodical to replace one that was never complete or has been broken by loss or damage during years of use.

Making the choices

The basic decisions about preservation policy ultimately depend upon the answers given, whether locally, regionally or nationally, to the questions that we have suggested. Such a policy, preferably embodied in a document available to all relevant personnel in the library, cannot determine decisions, but it can help to determine the limits within which individual decisions are to be taken. These may be about particular books or documents, or whole classes of material defined by age, subject, use or other agreed criteria. In special cases, reference to the policy document is the ultimate justification for the conclusion that is reached. It ensures a reasonable degree of consistency, not merely of preservation activities, but in ensuring such activities are within the overall objectives of the library or archive.

A number of complex typologies of preservation decision-making have been suggested (Atkinson 1986; Child 1986), and guidelines have been published for the development and implementation of preservation policies, some of which are listed in Appendix 1 to this chapter. In a simplified form such typologies are helpful. The schemes proposed in Table 4.1, derived in part from a proposal made by a former Director of Preservation Services at the British Library (Clements 1987a), relate use and priority to the action to be taken.

Table 4.1 *Preservation decisions: a simplified typology*

Use	Priority	Action
High	High	Preserve/replace
Moderate	High	Preserve/replace
Low	High	Preserve
High	Moderate	Preserve/replace
Moderate	Moderate	Preserve
Low	Moderate	Preserve/substitute
High	Low	Preserve
Moderate	Low	Substitute/dispose
Low	Low	Dispose

The terms high, moderate and low can only be very generally defined, although circulation statistics, local surveys of use and so on may help to assign specific numerical values. 'Priority' is most systematically defined in terms of the considerations and factors that were discussed earlier in this chapter. Despite the need for specific institutional definitions, however, the essential relationships can be generalized. A few examples may help to illustrate both the utility and the limitations of such an approach. These examples are illustrated in Table 4.2.

Table 4.2 *Some preservation decisions: an outline guide*

Category	Use	Priority	Life	Condition	Decision
Public library: popular fiction	High	High	5 years	Poor	Rebind or replace
Research library: newspapers	Low	High	∞	Moderate/Poor	Make or buy surrogate and store original
	Medium	High	∞	Poor	Make or buy surrogate Conserve and store original
Special library: journals	Medium	High	2 years	Well-used	Protect
Academic library: student text	High	High	3-5 years	Damaged by use	Repair or replace
University library: first edition of literary work	Moderate or Low	Moderate, but becoming High	>10 years but later ∞	Light damage, but increasing financial value	Conserve and consider for transfer to closed access or special collections

As a first example, and incidentally to illustrate the pervasiveness of preservation in so many aspects of librarianship, let us return to the case of a popular novel in the lending stock of a public library. If selection has been effective, this is in the high use category, but would not normally be regarded as a high priority for preservation. On the other hand, there are other considerations to be taken into account in defining priority, especially if we follow the practice of one leading expert and substitute the term 'value', which he takes 'to include bibliographic, aesthetic and financial factors' (Clements 1986). If the library's policy is to retain such fiction in the general lending stock for, say, five years and if that is expected to generate, say, 200 loans, then its preservation for that time, in a condition which permits that level of use, is indeed a high priority. It therefore falls into the high use/high priority category, which effectively dictates permanent availability either by preservation or by replacement. As the book reaches the end of its desired life, however, it changes category. Towards the end of the five-year period it has probably reached the moderate use/moderate priority category, and replacement is less likely to be considered. If it is earmarked for disposal at the end of its life, preservation at this stage may take the form of little more than running repairs carried out by unskilled junior staff. If, on the other hand, it is destined to be sent to a reserve store for more or less permanent retention, then more active steps may be needed at the time of its relegation to ensure its continued survival in a usable condition. This might suggest the low use/moderate priority level of action.

Just as public libraries are sometimes assumed, even by their own managers, not to be involved in preservation activities, so it is commonly thought that research libraries seek to preserve everything. Both assumptions are fallacious. In practice, most material in research libraries falls into the low use category. That which does not is, in general, reference material of the kind that is heavily used and readily available in many libraries. Nevertheless, even low use material, if it is important for research, has to be preserved in some form. Replacement by acquiring another copy is, generally speaking, very difficult; and if older books are involved, as they often are, this may entail high direct and indirect costs in locating and purchasing a copy. In the case of unique items, which, by definition, includes all manuscript documents, replacement is of course impossible. The low use/low priority category is effectively excluded from consideration in such a library since disposal is not normally an acceptable course of action for material of this kind. In practice, the choice is between preservation or substitution on the one hand, and the creation of a surrogate followed by minimal passive measures to preserve the original on the other. Newspapers, in particular, because they are so difficult to preserve and to store (and often in very poor condition), have until recently been the main priority for surrogate creation programmes in Britain and many other countries. They could be argued to fall into the low use/moderate priority category suggested here, leaving the low use/high priority ranking for those items for which a surrogate is not acceptable because the book or document is itself an historic object. This is indeed a major issue in the preservation of newspapers (IFLA Working Group on Newspapers 1988). There are, however, no easy answers, and even major research libraries have long since begun to reconsider their commitment to total preservation. This was the thrust of the Enright Report (Enright, Hellinga and Leigh 1989), which helped to redefine the British Library's collection and retention policies.

Conclusions

It should always be remembered that the objective of a preservation policy is to make information available to users by selecting for preservation the material in which information is stored. It is neither desirable nor possible to preserve everything. Even national libraries have to be selective; a recent proposal from the British Library suggests that selectivity will become an even more significant element of collection management and preservation policies in that institution (British Library 1993: 21–7). The pressures for selectivity, however, both there and elsewhere, are not only financial or space-related. There are also sound professional and intellectual reasons for relating the size and quality of the stock to the demands and needs of the users, and doing so with a proper consideration of information resources available from elsewhere. National policies for preservation, like national policies for information development in general, are the context in which local and institutional decisions have to be taken. It has been forcefully argued that the availability of high-quality interlending services can assist not only in providing rapid access to information, but also in preserving the information itself (Line 1988). The sharing of resources was the starting-point for the evolution of the Conspectus concept, and has become the driving force behind a number of important preservation initiatives, especially in the high-cost area of surrogate creation. We shall return to this in Chapter 7, for inter-institutional cooperation, local, national and international, is a key area of preservation policy implementation.

Further reading

There is surprisingly little literature dealing at a general level with the subject of this chapter, but the relevant parts of Harvey (1993) are excellent. See also the papers in National Preservation Office (forthcoming).

Chapter 5
THE PHYSICAL DIMENSION OF PRESERVATION

Introduction

An understanding of the use of books and information, both generally and in a particular library, is the necessary foundation of a preservation policy. Before a policy can be developed and implemented, however, there is another set of factors that needs to be considered. Preservation policy makes sense only if it is technically and economically realistic, so that until a library or archive has assessed the extent of its preservation needs it cannot meaningfully determine what its policy shall be. In turn, this leads to a consideration of what methods and materials are available, at what cost, to undertake the work needed. As we have seen, the preservation problem arises from two fundamental causes: first, there are the inherent properties and weaknesses of the materials used as information carriers; and secondly, there is the interaction between the materials and the environment in which they are stored and used. To provide the basic information upon which an institutional preservation policy can be built, it is necessary to make systematic surveys of both the library building and the contents of the building. The objective of the survey is to find out about existing conditions and to try to identify future difficulties, and then to put the results in a broader context of institutional objectives and external factors. That in turn leads to a consideration of the techniques available to both repair existing damage and minimize further damage.

The preservation survey: buildings

The preservation survey logically starts with the building, since that contains the environment in which most library and archive materials spend almost all of their time. It should always be remembered that, with the exception of the most heavily used items in the loan stock, library materials spend virtually their entire life not merely in the building, but actually on the shelf. It is there that deterioration starts; preservation has to follow its example. The building itself, and the various services needed to operate it (such as power, water, heating and cooling and telecommunications systems) have to be inspected in order to assess their possible impact on the preservation of library and archival materials. Although it is important to maintain a clear distinction between a preservation survey of a building and the sort of survey that might be undertaken by an architect or an engineer, there are also some important similarities. In essence, the building survey is a form of risk assessment, attempting to identify those aspects of the building and its services which are potentially hazardous or could be detrimental to the collections. The preservation survey will, no doubt, normally be under the supervision of a professional librarian or archivist, aware of the professional issues that arise from the conditions in which materials are stored, but the skills of other professionals will be needed in order to produce a comprehensive result.

The basic environmental hazards to library materials - temperature, humidity, light, air quality and biological infestation - dictate the form of the survey, which will seek to discover and evaluate both natural and man-made hazards. The starting-point is the general condition of the building as a whole. The concern is not so much to discover serious structural or material defects, but rather to assess the general suitability of the building for its purpose. The materials from which it is constructed – wood, brick or stone, for example – will affect weatherproofing and heat insulation. A flat roof can lead to difficulties with water seepage in heavy rain. Ill-fitting doors and windows can admit both water and animal life. These are basic facts with which the librarian has to live. Since they can be changed only by costly structural alterations, it is particularly important to be aware of them. Inside the building, the survey will look at matters that are perhaps rather more under the control of the librarian. Indeed, the depth and level of the survey are largely determined by the librarian. The requirements vary for different areas of the building, and the survey will reflect this. In particular, any preservation survey will be largely concentrated on storage areas used for materials of high value in the sense that they are a priority for long-term preservation.

The *temperature* and *humidity* of the storage areas are fundamental information; this is of course critical in areas used for housing materials of exceptional value, importance or fragility, or very vulnerable and sometimes volatile materials such as film. A preservation survey will seek to establish the typical conditions in different parts of the building, as well as noting the systems by which the building is heated, cooled and ventilated, how the systems are actually used, and how effective they are. A vital element here is whether there are effective monitoring systems, and how they are used. In critical areas (such as storage space for exceptionally valuable materials), monitoring should be on a daily basis. It may even be continuous, using thermometers and hygrometers which create a paper record of variations in temperature and relative humidity; in very sophisticated systems and exceptional circumstances, the environment is monitored by computers that give audible or visible warnings of unacceptable changes.

Air quality is another major area of concern for the survey. Again, measurements will have to be taken, and monitoring systems noted. Unlike systems for monitoring and controlling the ambient temperature, which are almost universal, monitoring of air quality is unusual, and control systems are found in fewer than one-fifth of British libraries (Feather, Matthews and Eden 1996: 66). In library and archive buildings which do not have full environmental control systems, there are inevitably some seasonal variations in temperature, humidity and air quality. This is especially true in those parts of the world where there are significant seasonal changes in the weather, such as a north European winter or a tropical rainy season. The initial survey, therefore, has to be carried out over a period of at least one year, and also has to take into account any freak conditions in that year, such as an unusually harsh winter or an exceptionally hot summer.

The means and intensity of *lighting* also have to be noted. This includes any measures that have been taken to protect materials from such hazards as direct light, and the use of filtered light sources where these are appropriate. Since light levels should always be as low as possible in storage areas, the use of switches that automatically turn off the lights after a predetermined period, unless they are reset, should also be noted.

Finally, the survey will have an assessment, necessarily subjective, of the general cleanliness and tidiness of the storage areas, and there will be an inspection for signs of animal droppings, which might indicate the presence in the building of rodents or other *biological infestation*. Special areas within the building, such as those used for exhibitions, will be the subject of special inspections, as will the exhibition cases themselves, where micro-environments exist and can be modified and controlled (Cunha 1988; Cunha, Lowell and Schnare 1982; Motylewski 1991).

Even in closed-access non-circulating collections, materials do not spend all their time either on the shelf in the stack or on users' desks. They travel between stacks and reading areas, and may be sent to and from the bindery or the photographic studio. They are received in an accessions area and pass through cataloguing areas. Although the environmental conditions in such places are not of such critical concern as those in storage areas, since the materials are in only fairly short-term transit, it is important that the procedures used for transportation and handling are consistent with the needs of preservation. The design of book trolleys, the size of cataloguers' desks and the areas available for storage of books and manuscripts in a photographic studio are among the many concerns of the preservation survey.

The preservation survey: collections

The inspection of the building is only the first stage of the initial preservation survey and arguably the less important. There follows the survey of the collections themselves, for whose protection the whole programme is to be designed. Even in a comparatively small library it is normally impossible to inspect every item. Survey techniques have to be used to examine a statistically valid sample of holdings, so that it is possible to form an acceptably accurate overall impression of the condition and needs of the entire collection. The precise method will vary according to the size and nature of the institution and its holdings, but the normal pattern would be to examine items selected by using a table of random numbers, ensuring that all parts of the collection and storage areas are sampled in this way. Where the collection can be divided into discrete elements which may have different preservation needs - manuscripts and printed books, for example - each element will be separately subjected to the same technique. It is particularly important to undertake a survey of the highest priority categories of material. Moreover, such a survey is not a one-off operation; ideally, there should be a regular cycle of inspection, so that the entire collection is inspected on a regular basis, a practice which is common but by no means universal in libraries (Feather, Matthews and Eden 1996: 60–3).

A general preservation survey cannot reveal minute details about every book or document. It merely records fairly generalized impressions of the overall condition of the collections, and so there is, inevitably, an element of subjectivity. It is for this reason that the sampling technique is so important; it is the only truly objective criterion in the survey. The staff who undertake a preservation survey need appropriate understanding of the field; indeed, ideally they should be either trained conservators or professional librarians or archivists with some knowledge of conservation. If professional staff are not available, some basic training can be given to others so that they can at least recognize major indicators of preservation problems such as mould, water damage or damp, embrittlement and active insects, as well as any signs of damage by excessive or careless use, and more general indicators such as dirt or general deterioration of paper and bindings.

The normal practice is to record this data on standard forms which can then be collated (Figure 5.1). It is through such sample surveys that the full extent of the preservation problem in the world's libraries and archives has been gradually revealed. In

Britain, surveys are neither as common nor as comprehensive as they should be, although there have been more than the literature reveals (Matthews 1995).

A survey of the collection provides the essential data needed for the planning of future action. Particular attention is obviously paid to materials that fall into the high priority category; indeed, in a particularly important collection, it may be desirable to inspect the contents item by item. This is very time-consuming; it may well be justified only when a collection has already been identified from the general survey as a priority for conservation work. In other words, it is high priority material in generally poor condition which is inspected in this way. At this stage, it is essential that the survey is conducted by an expert, preferably a professional conservator, for more details now have to be recorded, including specific statements about condition and some preliminary notes on the proposed treatment. There are even some particular tests which can be carried out if the importance and general state of the material is considered to justify this. These might include testing for acidity and embrittlement.

The level of acidity is measured in pH (potential of hydrogen) units. The pH of a substance is equal to the common logarithm of the reciprocal of the concentration of hydrogen ions in moles per decilitre of sulution. Measurement requires the use of the appropriate instrument, a pH meter, which records the relative proportions of acid and alkali in the paper. A pH level of >7 is acidic, and a level of <7 is alkaline; pure water has a pH level of 7, and is chemically neutral. Instruments are available from all conservation supply firms, and are easy to use.

The measurement of embrittlement is a different and slightly more controversial matter, because of the intrusive and potentially damaging application of the so-called 'fold test'. This involves folding the corner of a leaf backwards and forwards along the same line until it breaks. As a general rule, paper is considered to be embrittled if this break takes place after six or fewer folds. Obviously, if a book is discovered to be embrittled, then it suffers further damage when the paper breaks during this test; even if it is not, the leaf chosen for testing is weakened. The fold test is a useful device, but it is one to be applied sparingly and only by those with appropriate skills and knowledge. It is necessary only when embrittlement seems likely to be a major problem. Since it is a consequence of the breakdown of the fibres in acidic paper, other tests of acidity, such as pH measurement, or even simple observation of the browning of the paper, are to be preferred, at least in the first instance. It is also worth remembering that in Britain, so far as we know, embrittlement is not the predominant preservation problem that it is in the United States.

The purpose of the survey

Before undertaking a preservation survey, it is essential to define its purpose. In particular, if it has already been decided that the collection is to be preserved in the original format, then the survey will primarily be directed towards determining the appropriate repair or restoration work to be undertaken on each book. If, on the other hand, it has been agreed that surrogates are acceptable if they are necessary, or that replacement is suitable if it is possible, then the designation of which items can be repaired and which will have to be substituted is one of the objectives of the survey itself. In such a case the actual details of the work to be undertaken need be specified only for those items on which conservation work is thought to be desirable.

A possible model for a book report form for a preliminary survey can be found in Figure 5.1. There will, of course, be local variations to the form according to the nature of the collection, the funding available for the survey (and indeed for subsequent conservation work) and the skill and knowledge of the staff available to undertake the survey. In essence, however, this form records all that needs to be known in the first instance. Much of what is recorded here may seem to be a little vague but, if the staff are given clear instructions, this is not a major problem. For example, if a distinction is to be maintained between 'broken' hinges – meaning that the board is detached – and 'weak' hinges – meaning that the board is still attached but in danger of coming away – that can be fully explained and then consistently applied. It requires no great technical knowledge and the terminology is unambiguous. It is only when a more detailed survey is undertaken of high priority materials that more detailed technical records need to be created; for that, of course, high levels of expertise are essential.

Using the surveys

The purpose of the preservation surveys of the building and its contents is to provide information upon which managerial decisions about policy can be soundly based.

Buildings

In the case of the library building itself, three areas of policy need to be considered:

* a maintenance programme
* security arrangements
* risk assessment and management.

A **maintenance programme** is an integral part of the operational activities of any organization that occupies a building for which it is responsible. For a library or an archive building, however, there are some special considerations. The internal environment is so important that continuous monitoring is probably desirable, at least in areas in which high priority materials are stored and used. This means monitoring the temperature, humidity and air quality, and then using whatever means are available for regulating them to achieve the desired conditions. The preservation policy will prescribe both the levels to be maintained, and the regularity of the monitoring. It is also important, in this as in other aspects of preservation policy, that a proper reporting mechanism is established, so that if maintenance staff discover a problem the facts are made known as soon as possible to the librarian or archivist responsible for the preservation management programme. In any case, reports of the readings from the monitoring devices ought to be made available to the manager on a regular basis.

The criteria to be applied have already been discussed (see pp.34–47); these ideal standards cannot always be attained, except perhaps in new buildings, where appropriate conditions should be an integral part of the design brief for the architect and the building services engineer (Briggs 1994; Hookham 1994). Even in older buildings, however, some adaptation will be needed, for it has to be recognized that material intended for permanent preservation will survive only if good conditions can be provided. This is particularly true of the more sensitive materials such as film. It is also, however, important to recognize that there is a vital distinction to be made between storage areas and other parts of the building. A new

```
CONSERVATION SURVEY

BOOK REPORT FORM

Shelfmark.........   Date of report.........
```

	Condition	Work needed
BINDING: hinges		
boards		
spine		
cover		
sewing		
PAPER: pH level		
embrittled		
mould		
insect damage		
water damage		
fire damage		
heat damage		
mutilated		
annotations		
other		

Figure 5.1 *Conservation Survey: Book Report Form*

standard on storage of library and archival material, at present under development by the International Standards Organisation (Committee ISO/TC46/SC10), explicitly excludes areas to which the public are admitted, and books that are available for use outside the library. This distinction is to be welcomed, for it puts the need to maintain the highest standards of storage into the proper context. Once a library or archive has identified those collections and documents for which preservation is regarded as essential, it can take appropriate steps to provide the appropriate conditions. The storage area may vary from an entire building to a part of a book stack, or may be no more than a single room or even a sealed cupboard with its own environmental control systems.

Whatever its extent, however, it has to be accepted that an area in which high priority material is stored is itself a high priority for the installation, operation and monitoring of environmental control systems, and for regular maintenance and repair. Particular attention must be paid to potential hazards revealed by the building survey. If materials are stored close to possible sources of water leakage, for example, regular checks are needed to ensure that no such problems have occurred, and steps should be taken to move valuable materials to more appropriate storage.

Security arrangements are an integral part of a preservation policy. Damage to books, even by proper use, is caused by people as much as by natural hazards, but most of that is accidental or careless. Occasionally, however, theft or deliberate damage do take place. Neither can wholly be prevented, but adequate and reasonable security arrangements are essential.

Theft is a danger that cannot be ignored in any library. For research libraries and archives containing material with a high commercial value, it is especially important to take steps to prevent it, but the need is not confined to them. Security measures may include the vetting of potential users, the guarding of exits by security officers or electronic systems, and the searching or deposit of bags and other containers (Thomas 1987: 19, 24). The usual anti-theft precautions are either bag checks or, most commonly today, electronic 'tagging' of books. In such systems, a magnetized strip is inserted invisibly into the book; the strip is desensitized when the item is properly checked out through the circulation system. If it is not desensitized, it sets off an alarm when carried through the electronic gates at the exit. Such systems are not cheap, but they are almost infallible and could be argued to be very cost-effective.

Although theft can never be eliminated, it can be reduced to an insignificant level. Thefts of valuable or important material should be reported to the police, and in both Britain and the USA reporting systems have been developed by librarians and antiquarian booksellers (who also suffer badly from theft) to circulate the details of stolen books, thereby preventing their resale (Allen 1995). The guidelines developed in the USA have been published by the Rare Books and Manuscripts Section of the Association of College and Research Libraries (RBMS Security Committee 1990), while a British equivalent is in the final stages of development by a joint working party of the Antiquarian Booksellers Association and the Rare Books Group of the Library Association. Serious professional theft for commercial purposes is most likely to be of older and rarer materials. It is, however, worth remembering that many such thefts have been from libraries with little-used collections of older books, as well as theft by not returning borrowed materials. In such circumstances, security is sometimes lax, since that part of the collection is not a high priority. To compound the difficulty, it may be a long time before the theft is actually discovered, and there is sometimes a reluctance among both librarians and the governing bodies of libraries to admit that theft has taken place. Finally, a few very high-profile institutions, especially in politically unstable regions, may also feel that precautions have to be taken against possible acts of terrorism.

Security, however, also embraces controlling damage to materials and is much more difficult than theft prevention. Minute supervision of reading areas is impossible in all but the most specialized cases. In a large research library, the main reading room can rarely be supervised in detail; even reading rooms for rare books and manuscripts may be subject to little more than general scrutiny. Lending libraries have a far greater problem, as do those libraries in which continuous supervision of public areas is impossible for architectural or economic reasons. The mutilation of books is all too common in both public and academic libraries. Cursory checks when books are returned from loan may reveal the damage, but not the culprit. Exhortation is probably the only practical solution to this problem, and that has obvious limitations. Avoiding or preventing loss or damage is an important part of any preservation programme.

Underlying both building maintenance and security arrangements is **risk assessment and management**. The term comes from the insurance industry, but the ideas it represents have been present in the professional thinking of librarians and archivists for many years. Traditionally, it has been called 'disaster planning', 'disaster management' or 'disaster preparedness planning'. Whatever the words, the concepts are essentially the same: if potential risks can be identified and their probability assessed, steps can be taken to eliminate or minimize them while putting in place a contingency plan for determining what to do if preventative measures fail or, in general terms, some unpredicted (and perhaps unpredictable) event takes place.

The preparation of a disaster control plan has become a key element in preservation policy-making during the last few years. In Britain, however, it made a slow start. The questionnaire for the Ratcliffe inquiry did not even ask specifically about disaster plans (Ratcliffe 1984: 76-8); nor did that for a world-wide survey sponsored by Unesco, IFLA and ICA in 1986 (Clements 1987b: Annexe 1). A survey in 1986 revealed that only 6.6% of a large sample of libraries and archives in England, Wales and Northern Ireland had a disaster plan, and only a further 3.7% were engaged in compiling one (Tregarthen Jenkin 1987: 2). The most recent and most comprehensive British study shows that about 20% of the respondents to a wide-ranging survey had such plans in 1995 (Matthews and Eden 1996: 6). The pioneer of disaster planning in the UK was the National Library of Scotland, whose published version of its knowledge and experience, dating from 1985, remains an invaluable source for all those involved in disaster preparedness (Anderson and McIntyre 1985). Work began much earlier in the United States. The first significant published guide there dates from as long ago as 1978 (Bohem 1978). A Unesco study produced an invaluable document (Buchanan 1988), and the recent British study has also generated important and very practical guidelines for the development and implementation of a policy and plan (Matthews and Eden 1996).

The building survey is the starting-point for the disaster control plan, since it reveals the building's inherent hazards from water and fire, the two most likely causes of large-scale disasters in temperate climates. Such hazards abound in modern buildings; they are found in water-based heating and cooling systems, as well as the plumbing of lavatories, drinking-water supplies, and so on. Above all, however, we have to look at the vastly complicated electrical systems and installations used for lighting, air-conditioning systems, and the operation of equipment such as lifts, photographic apparatus, binding machinery, microform readers and computers. Certain rooms or areas can also be identified as being particularly hazardous. These include computer rooms, binderies, conservation laboratories, photographic studios, kitchens and any part of the building where smoking is allowed. There may also be temporary hazards created from time to time by building works, and indeed by workmen. At least one major library fire is believed to have been caused by a smouldering cigarette butt dropped by a workman engaged in roof repair work. To some extent, all of these hazards can be anticipated by installing monitoring devices such as smoke, heat and fire detectors, and regular monitoring of them. In addition, essential safety regulations relating to electrical apparatus and other potential hazards should be meticulously enforced.

Away from the comparatively benign climatic conditions of north-west Europe, other hazards also need to be taken into account. These include earthquakes, monsoons, hurricanes, forest or bush fires and similar natural occurrences. In general terms, these are predictable. We do not know exactly when they are going to happen, but it is possible to make reasonable estimates of the probability of their happening eventually. Indeed, some of them can be considered when the building is being designed. In some parts of the world, for example, building regulations prescribe the maximum height and minimum strength of buildings erected in earthquake zones. Unlike these events, however, human error or malice cannot be predicted. Arson has been the cause of a number of major library fires in recent years.

Although disaster *prevention* is the best remedy, disaster *preparedness* is the best response to the unpredictable and the unpreventable. The disaster plan essentially dictates what shall be done and, just as importantly, who shall be responsible for doing it, if a disaster occurs. The general pattern in larger libraries is to assign responsibility for the design and execution of the plan to a senior member of the library staff, and then to establish a committee which develops and implements the plan. In smaller libraries, responsibility normally rests with one individual, often the head of the library. An important element in the implementation stage is staff training, so that everyone knows what to do if disaster strikes. It should be remembered that disasters are not confined to working hours, and out-of-hours contacts and telephone numbers are a key element of the plan. So too is liaison with local emergency services and especially with the fire brigade, which is the first line of defence against both fire and flood. It has to be recognized, of course, that if a fire breaks out when the building is occupied, evacuation is the first priority. The means of achieving this are also a part of the disaster planning process. Indeed, periodic unannounced fire drills are invaluable both as a test of the evacuation procedures and as a form of staff training.

If a disaster should occur, nothing can be done until the immediate crisis is passed, especially in the case of fire. It is the next stage that is critical to the rescue and survival of books and documents. Water damage is both the most insidious and the most likely consequence of any disaster. Drying of sodden materials is essential if they are to have any chance of survival; industrial-scale deep freezing may be necessary if items cannot be treated immediately, but this merely defers the solution rather than solving the problem. Part of the disaster planning process is to discover where such facilities are available, and to make contingency plans for their use in an emergency. Fire-damaged materials are even more difficult to rehabilitate than water-damaged items, and specialist advice will have to be sought. The disaster plan will include the names of such specialists as well as lists of organizations, individuals and companies that may be needed during the rescue and recovery period (Matthews and Eden 1996).

Collections

The survey of the collections as a whole, and of individual items within them, is intended to reveal the need for preservation and conservation. This is then related to the broader priorities established by other means.

The preservation policy defines the general outlines of the actions to be taken in regard to damaged or endangered items, in particular in three areas:

- preventative measures
- binding and other repair work
- format conversion.

Preventative measures are a key element in any preservation management policy. Indeed, much of the earlier part of this section has been concerned with precisely that: reducing the likelihood of damage, loss or destruction. At the level of the individual item, other measures can be taken.

Many forms of protection are available for library materials in addition to binding. For many books it is both cheap and efficient to use the purpose-made boxes that have become an important instrument of preservation in the recent years. The 'phase box' (so called because it is, in theory, a temporary expedient) is a made-to measure box, constructed of acid-free or chemically inert card, designed to protect the book both on the shelf and in transit between the shelf and the reader's desk. It is made of a single piece of card, with a hinged lid, and sometimes with ties to ensure that the book cannot fall out when the box is removed from the shelf. Some manufacturing systems use sophisticated technology to produce a box which is a perfect fit (Waters 1995). Phase boxes are comparatively cheap to make, costing as little as about £15.00 for one suitable for an 18th century octavo of 200 or so pages. Consequently, large numbers of books can be protected for a fraction of the cost of full conservation of the same items. Boxes may be used either where the book needs protection until the time comes for full-scale repairs (the original 'phase' concept) or because it may be undesirable to resew or rebind, in order to preserve historical or bibliographical evidence. In practice, however, these phase boxes have probably become the only, and therefore permanent, means of protecting large numbers of older books.

There are many variations on the phase box itself, and other manifestations of the principle of taking temporary, or allegedly temporary, measures to prevent further damage and deterioration. These include 'book shoes', which are slip cases that protect the covers of the book while being open at the spine; they are particularly suitable for use in libraries where the appearance of the shelves is important. Boxes, slip cases and portfolios can all be made from acid-free card, or from card covered in book cloth. Even the latter is cheaper than a full binding, and can be lettered on the spine to make it aesthetically acceptable. Even cheaper than these expedients, and an essential first-aid measure, is the use of linen tape to hold together a book whose boards are detached or loose. The tape is tied around the book in both directions, and loosely secured with a bow knot; it can then stand on the shelf without any danger of further loss. With a little more time and effort, damaged books can be wrapped in acid-free paper and tied in tape.

All of these measures fall a long way short of the ideal, but when budgets are small (and they will not get any larger in the foreseeable future), skilled work is expensive (and skilled workers are not always available), and the problem is both urgent and large scale, they can be adopted on the principle that something which can prevent or inhibit further damage and is not itself damaging is better than nothing at all. Increasingly, preventive measures are being adopted, and any preservation management policy and programme will take full advantage of them. None of them precludes more permanent measures being taken at some later date, and none will exacerbate existing damage.

It should be added that not all boxes are temporary measures. They can be used as permanent protection for books of particular value or aesthetic interest. Books in fine bindings or other bindings of exceptional historical significance are obvious candidates for this treatment. In such cases, the boxes will, of course, be purpose-made to ensure that the fit is exact, and the book will neither be too tightly contained in the box nor able to slide about inside it. The box may well be lined with foam or some other soft material. For a handful of the most important books, a wooden box may be appropriate. This solution is sometimes adopted for medieval manuscripts and other large books to provide maximum protection for irreplaceable artefacts (Hadgraft 1994).

Binding and other repair work is needed when it is considered that damaged items have to be kept in their original physical format. Many options are available; which is adopted for a particular book will be determined by a number of factors including the cost of the treatment, the significance of the book itself and its likely use. For recently acquired materials, some preventative work may be justified before it is even added to stock, if it will lengthen its useful life. The widespread practice of strengthening paperbacks is one well-known example; the use of temporary binders for the short-term protection of individual issues of heavily-used periodicals is another. The regular binding of completed volumes of periodicals is also a common practice, and is certainly justified where a high-use periodical is expected to continue to be in demand for some time after publication. Individual decisions on such matters are most effectively taken within the broad guidelines of an agreed policy, and will be discussed at length in Chapter 6.

The preservation or conservation of older materials presents more complex issues. Libraries with significant collections of older material, or indeed of any material with a high preservation priority, typically create special storage areas, and perhaps distinct administrative arrangement, for these materials. The special collections department is central to the preservation strategy for research materials. In British and American academic and research libraries, this section (variously named, and sometimes subdivided) would normally include all books printed before a particular date (1800 and 1850 are perhaps the most common), manuscript materials and analogous materials such as typescripts, and, depending on the library and it collections, such things as modern fine printing and private press books, prints and other graphic material, maps, sheet music, newspapers and collections of particular institutional interest. In a public library, the latter would always include the local studies and local history collections.

Special collections are normally housed in closed access storage – although some parts of local studies collections in public libraries may not be – and are non-circulating. This affords them protection from both damage and theft, and also allows the creation of an appropriate environment in which they can be stored. Consultation takes place under controlled – and usually supervised – conditions, and there are often special regulations in relation to photocopying and such comparatively trivial but nonetheless important matters as the use of pencil rather than pen for note-taking. Although all the library's holdings are included in the broad sweep of the preservation policy, it is almost certain that the bulk of the specialist work will be in special collections.

Within special collections, decisions have to be taken about priorities for preservation, and about appropriate methods. Repairs should not be undertaken at random, but within broad policy guidelines. The policy should also prescribe the acceptable techniques and materials. A wide range of options is available. As has been suggested the use of phase boxes, portfolios and slip-cases is probably the most commonly adopted: it is quick and cheap, and affords enough protection for low-use material. When a book is badly damaged, however, or is of some particular interest, value or importance, repairs will be needed, and will have to be undertaken by properly trained workers. Many libraries, especially in the academic sector, still have their own binderies, and it is desirable that all work on special collections is carried out there. Libraries without these facilities have to make use of commercial binders, and indeed much good work is done in the commercial sector.

Regardless of who does the work or where it is done, the relationship between the librarians or archivists on the one hand and the binder and conservator on the other is central. The two must work together, recognizing and respecting each other's areas of expertise. The librarian takes the professional decisions: priorities for binding and repair, acceptable techniques, desirable materials, and so on. The binder or conservator advises on the appropriateness of particular techniques or materials, the likely cost of the work, and the suitability of particular courses of action. In the end, however, it is the librarian or archivist – as both owner of the books and commissioner of the work on them – who takes the decisions.

There are two aspects to the repair of damaged books: bindings and paper. A book which has lost its binding altogether, or whose binding is irreparably damaged, will normally be rebound. This process involves resewing the gatherings and then constructing a new craft binding. Ideally, this should be covered in material appropriate to the age of the book (such as leather), although no attempt is being made to deceive or to do anything beyond providing a functional and acceptable means of preserving the text-block. As a general rule, all work on historical materials – books and manuscripts alike – should be based on the principle that as much as possible of the original should be preserved. This might mean, for example, replacing the spine strip of a book with new leather, but using the original boards and their leather covering, perhaps after some minor repairs and refurbishment. In any case, nothing should be done which causes the loss of historical and bibliographical evidence, such as marks of former ownership and other annotations. For many books, something short of a full rebinding is both the cheapest and the most appropriate option; for all books and documents of artefactual value, however, ethical factors are paramount (Baynes-Cope 1994).

The repair of paper is a more complex matter. As we have seen, paper undergoes chemical change as well as physical damage, and some of the chemical processes are inherent to the paper itself and the materials of which it is made (see pp.17–23). Where the source of the damage is specific and identifiable, some action may be possible, but it has to be emphasized that very high levels of expertise are needed for work of this kind. Archival documents and other manuscripts have to be assessed and treated individually (Bell 1994), although some general principles can be enunciated.

A matter which is always urgent is the presence of active biological pests, such as insects and fungi. This will require specialist treatment to kill the organisms, often involving fumigation in a sealed chamber. Such work can only be undertaken in laboratory conditions, and is the province of experts employed for the purpose. The key indicator of insect activity is the presence of recent droppings either in the book or on the shelf beneath or behind it, which should be revealed by the preservation survey.

Biological damage is comparatively uncommon in temperate climates, but it is a major hazard in tropical and sub-tropical countries, and in buildings that are too hot and whose RH is too high in whatever climatic zone they are located. A more common problem, however, is dealing with the results of past insect activity or fungal growth, as well as with the damage caused to paper by use and by exposure to heat and light. Badly damaged paper can be repaired by a number of techniques. The traditional methods used by the conservator involve the use of a thin, chemically neutral, paper called 'Japanese tissue'. A small piece is cut almost to shape around the damaged area, and attached using a suitable adhesive; the extraneous tissue is then carefully removed with a scalpel, repairing the gap in the paper or, perhaps most commonly, restoring a strong straight edge to a damaged leaf. This is slow work, but it is one of the basic skills of the conservator. To some extent, it is, however, being displaced by the leaf-casting technique, in which the damaged leaf is immersed in a bath of pulp, constituted to the highest modern standards of papermaking (Petherbridge 1987); the pulp adheres to the existing leaf around any holes or at the damaged edges, thus reconstituting the leaf. The technique takes less than five minutes for each leaf treated; the large capital investment in the equipment can therefore soon be offset by the cost-effectiveness of the process itself.

In conserving a single book, whether printed or manuscript, the full process will normally involve stripping down the original binding (or the remains of it), repairing the paper, resewing and rebacking and rebinding. For some items of great importance, this work may occupy a conservator for many weeks; even the external design of the binding may be matter of concern. For most books, however, the work can be undertaken comparatively quickly, although it should always be done by properly trained personnel, and to the specifications of the librarian or archivist.

While bindings can be repaired only on an individual and hand-craft basis, there are some aspects of work on paper that can be partially mechanized and even undertaken on a large scale. Leaf-casting is the most important example of the former; the area that has been most fully explored for potential large-scale techniques is that of deacidification. As we have seen (see pp.5–6), the embrittlement of paper because of the oxidization of its acid content is one of the major preservation problems in libraries and archives containing material from the second half of the 19th and first half of the 20th centuries. The sheer scale of the problem has inevitably led to a search for solutions on a comparable scale and to the development of mass deacidification processes.

An acceptable deacidification process must meet three basic criteria:

- the acid must be neutralized
- a 'buffer' of alkali must be created to prevent future acidification
- there must be no side-effects that will damage the paper or other materials, and no unacceptable chemical residue in the treated paper.

In addition, it is desirable that the process also strengthens the paper by catalysing a chemical reaction that will strengthen the molecular structure of the fibres.

Experiments to create such processes began in the 1970s. All work on a similar principle: the neutralizing agent, as a liquid or a gas, is brought into contact with the acidic paper for a predetermined length of time. This takes place in a sealed chamber, from which the chemical residues created by the process are subsequently removed including, in some cases, partial recovery of the deacidification agent itself. A large number of books (ideally several hundreds) can be treated simultaneously if the chamber is large enough. There are some drawbacks: most of the chemicals used are hazardous, and some are flammable or explosive; the chamber in some processes is a vacuum and the treated materials have to be brought back slowly to atmospheric pressure; in all the processes in which the chemical agent is in liquid form, the treated material has to be dried.

A number of processes has now been developed and tested, and although none is perfect, several are acceptable. Probably the greatest institutional contributor to the work has been the Library of Congress, whose Diethyl Zinc (DEZ) process was the first mass deacidification method to be used in the 1970s. Unlike all the subsequent processes, it uses the deacidifying agent in gaseous form, although this in itself created many early problems, including major hazards − DEZ spontaneously combusts on contact with air − and environmentally unacceptable waste products. To some extent, however, these have been overcome, and the DEZ process is still favoured by the Library of Congress (Harris and Shahani 1995).

There are now at least seven liquid-based processes that have been developed and tested. The first of these was the Wei T'o process (named after the traditional inventor of paper), which has been used for some years in the National Archives of Canada and elsewhere. Along with five other techniques, DEZ and Wei T'o were submitted to a formal evaluation programme at the Institut Royal du Patrimoine Artistique in Brussels between 1990 and 1992 (Liérnardy 1994). The results are summarized in Table 5.1, to which have been added a summary of characteristics of an eighth process − Battelle − developed in Germany in the late 1980s, and now installed in the Deutches Bibliothek, Leipzig (Liers and Schwerdt 1995; Wittekind 1994). The Belgian programme tested all the essential characteristics that librarians and archivists seek from a deacidification process, including not only the basic requirements listed, but also such issues as residual odour and observable colour change in the paper. The conclusion was that the DEZ and Bookkeeper processes were the best, followed by Wei T'o, the Sablé method and FMC, and that BPA and the Vienna method were not acceptable (the Battelle method was not part of this evaluation). A further study, sponsored by the European Commission on Preservation and Access, is to take place during 1996, and will produce a report intended to assist those handling programmes in libraries and archives. (Epic News 1996).

Mass deacidification is now beyond the experimental stage. Major libraries and archives have accepted it into the armoury of preservation and conservation tools, and its importance can only increase, for it is the best tool we have to combat one of the most common and insidious forms of damage to paper. Economic problems remain – the techniques are expensive, especially in terms of the capital costs of building the plants – and some further scientific refinement may be desirable. The battle is not yet won, but the weapons are available and the strategy in is place.

Despite the use of both age-old techniques of bookbinding, highly skilled conservation work and the results of modern scientific ingenuity, preservation of information in the original format is sometimes unnecessary and often impossible. **Format conversion** is our third major weapon. In Chapter 3, we considered one aspect of information preservation – electronic data – in which the only approach is to preserve selected data rather than to attempt to preserve the information carrier itself. The creation of document surrogates, however, is not confined to electronic data, and has indeed been a common practice for the last fifty years using the familiar technology of microfilm. Some photographic facsimiles of books were made in the late 19th century, but these were antiquarian and bibliophilic curiosities rather than tools of preservation, and, ironically, have now become important historical objects in their own right. The use of 35 mm monochrome film for the preservation of the information content of damaged or fragile material began in the 1930s when the New York Public Library initiated a major programme (see p.8). By the 1980s the creation of microform surrogates had become a major tool of preservation in both the United States and Europe, with major programmes being undertaken in a large number of libraries and archives.

Microfilming is increasingly associated with the preservation of newspapers, which are not only typically printed on very poor paper but are also in large formats that are difficult to store, transport and consult. Microfilming for preservation purposes, however, has its own standards and conventions which must be properly applied if the product is to be acceptable as an archival document. The highest standards of filming, processing and storage must be

Table 5.1 *Mass deacidification processes (Sources: Liénardy 1994; Liers and Schwerdt 1995)*

Process	Agent	Wet/Dry	Time	Test centre
Wei T'o	Magnesium methyl carbonate	wet	25 mins + drying	National Archives, Canada
Archival Aids	(1) Methoxy ethoxy magnesium carbonate (2) Ethoxy magnesium carbonate	wet	15–30 min + 24 h drying	Centre de recherches pour la conservation des documents graphiques, Sablé
Bookkeeper	Magnesium oxide	wet	10 min + 1 h	Preservation Technologies Inc
DEZ	Diethyl zinc	dry	8 h + 22 h recovery	Azko Chemicals Inc. for the Library of Congress
FMC	Magnesium butoxytriglycolate	wet	10 min + 3 h drying	FMC Corporation
BPA	Monodiethanolamine	wet	21 h	Fiber Preservation
Vienna method	Calcium hydroxide	wet	1 h + 3 days	Institut für Restaurierung, Vienna
Battelle method	Hexamethydisiloxane	wet	3 h	Deutches Bibliothek, Leipzig

met; these include BS5847 (British Standards Institution, 1980), and BS5699 (British Standards Institution, 1979). Other specifications have been published form time to time by the Library of Congress (Library of Congress 1982) and the British Library (National Preservation Office 1988). The processed film, however, must then be properly handled. The central principle is that the 'original' (known as the master negative) film (i.e. the processed negative that was in the camera) becomes an archival document. A copy negative (sometimes called an internegative) is used for the creation of subsequent generations of copies for use. The master negative itself is stored in optimal conditions, preferably on a different site from the document of which it is a surrogate. From the internegative, positive copies are generated for consultation (and perhaps sale), while the master negative lies undisturbed as a permanent record.

The creation of microfilm surrogates is not a cheap process, but it is effective and the technology of both manufacture and consultation is robust and familiar. Moreover, it has enough commercial potential to attract private sector interest. In the 1930s commercial microfilm was exploited by the newly founded University Microfilms Inc (now UMI) for the creation of a comprehensive series of films of English books printed before 1640, subsequently extended to 1700; in the hands of another company, similar projects now extend into the 18th and 19th centuries. These films not only made the very rare books which they reproduced more accessible than ever before, but also made an indirect contribution to the preservation of the originals by easing the pressure on them from potential users. There are comparatively few scholarly purposes for which the handling of the original is essential (Tanselle 1988); for the majority of users a high-quality surrogate is acceptable. At the same time, libraries with smaller collections of such materials can greatly increase the depth of their holdings by the use of these microform surrogates; the ends of both preservation and access are thus served.

The same argument applies to the increasingly common use of microfilm as a strategy for the preservation of the information content of newspapers. A film of a newspaper may even be able to offer the user something which no individual library can offer: a complete run. It also offers ease of consultation and wide availability. The Newsplan project in the UK was designed precisely to exploit this aspect of microfilm. On a regional basis, repositories of newspapers were inventoried, often creating a bibliographical record for the first time, with a view to subsequent filming of unique, rare or widely scattered items. Although the survey has made greater progress than the much more expensive process of actually creating the surrogates, the principle is well-established, and some filming has been done (Wresell 1994).

Once a copy of a printed document has been filmed to archival standards, there is no need to make another film. Unnecessary duplication has become a matter of concern, addressed in part by the creation of registers of microfilm masters. This practice began in the USA with the *National register of microforms*, and has subsequently been adopted in the British *Register of preservation microforms* and a European database, the *European register of microform masters* based at Göttingen University in Germany (Kuberek 1994). In at least one important case the creation of archival-standard films, and the entry of a record for the master negatives into the appropriate database, has been a condition of funding (Stagg 1995). The Mellon foundation injected an initial $2.5m into microfilming programmes at the British Library, the Bodleian Library, Oxford, and Cambridge University Library, followed by further benefactions with a wider scope (Kirtley 1992). The result of this benefaction has been to increase greatly the stock of archival microfilm in the UK, and to reiterate its importance as a mass preservation strategy for appropriate materials (Fox 1993). In the USA, the National Endowment for the Humanities administered more than $12m of federal funding for filming embrittled books in 1982 alone, and the whole project galvanized the preservation efforts of librarians and archivists (Farr 1992).

Microfilm is not, of course, the only available surrogate medium. Digitization is not yet widely used, but, as we have seen, it has real potential as a preservation medium, as well as having its own rather different preservation problems (see pp.51–77). For the present, however, digitization is no more than a technologically attractive experimental technique; microform, on the other hand, is a tried and tested technology that has already made a major contribution to the preservation problems of libraries and archives.

Conclusion

No one approach to preservation is comprehensive and sufficient for any library. Temporary protection, binding and rebinding, paper repair and the creation of document surrogates all have their part to play. The whole range of options needs to be considered; such consideration has to be in the context of institutional missions. The development of an agreed preservation policy is perhaps the most important step forward a library can take in making preservation a part of its normal management procedures. The policy has to be defined and agreed at the highest level in the institution, and command the general support of all those who will be involved with it. To be acceptable, it has to be based on the true needs of the institution. Some libraries may feel justified in preserving nothing, but even that decision has to be based on a proper consideration of the available information and of the implications of the decision. A policy to preserve everything, such as was alleged to exist in so many British libraries in the early 1980s, has even more significant implications which need to be understood. By considering the use, environment and physical condition of the collections, library managers will learn a great deal about the institutions in their care. Much of what is learned has implications far beyond the simplistic understanding (or rather misunderstanding) of preservation as being 'something to do with binding'. It impinges on library activities at every point from acquisition to disposal: it affects bibliographic record-keeping; it affects use; it affects policies relating to security, loans and users; it affects the design and maintenance of the building itself. Preservation is essential to the proper management of the library's most important material resource: its collection of media in which the information sought by its users is stored. The management of the preservation programme - the implementation of an agreed policy - is therefore one of the most important professional activities of the librarian or archivist.

Further reading

On all matters relating to preservation surveys, see Matthews (1995). A number of case studies has been published, many of them cited by Matthews. For a recent American perspective (although oriented towards museum work), see Getty Conservation Institute (1990). On buildings, see Dewe (1987), especially the chapter by Harry Faulkener-Brown (pp. 17-45). On security, see Burrows and Cooper (1992), Quinsee and Macdougall (1990), and Thomas (1987). On disaster management, see Matthews and Eden (1996). This includes a comprehensive bibliography, and guidelines on compiling a disaster control plan, for which also see Buchanan (1988). On recent trends in the use of preventive techniques and binding, see Fredericks (1992). On mass techniques, see Foot (1994). On preservation microfilming, see Gwynn (1987), currently in process of revision.

Chapter 6
PRESERVING INFORMATION: POLICY DEVELOPMENT AND IMPLEMENTATION

Introduction
An effective preservation policy depends, like any other aspect of management, upon the deployment of human, material and financial resources to meet agreed common objectives. In essence, the policy defines what is to be preserved, and what methods are to be employed in the preservation of particular classes of materials. It does so, however, in the context of the overall management of the institution and development of the collection, and of the conditions in which it is stored and used, as well as in relation to the availability of comparable information resources outside the institution. As an aspect of collection management, preservation is part of that continuous sequence of processes which begins with selection and ends with withdrawal or permanent retention. At a more mundane level, however, the implementation of policy-level preservation decisions depends upon the efficient administration of technical activities such as binding, repair and reprography. Finally, but of great importance, there is the human dimension which is integral to all management; in this case, that means the need for committed and properly trained staff at all levels.

Preservation policy: the elements
The development of a preservation policy at institutional level is ultimately dependent on the institution's mission. In some libraries, this might legitimately be a decision *not* to preserve material beyond a short period of intensive use. In other libraries, what is in effect a preservation policy may not be identified by that name, but forms a

125

part of a collection management and development policy. In most British libraries, even when there is a policy in place, there is no written version of it, although the practice of documenting policies is becoming more common (Feather, Matthews and Eden 1996: 52–4). In practice, most libraries have some sort of policy – even if it is only in the mind and memory of the librarian – about binding, repair and withdrawal of damaged or vulnerable material. How such a policy is described, and what it prescribes, is indeed an institutional concern. At a more general level, however, we can define the principal elements of a preservation policy in terms of issues to be addressed by library managers.

These issues can be summarized thus:

- **priorities** between categories of material or subdivisions of the collection
- acceptable **techniques and materials for repair**
- guidelines on **disposal**
- good practice in **storage and handling**
- regulations regarding **access and use**
- **disaster management and security** arrangements
- staff **training** and raising user awareness
- policies relating to **reprography and exhibitions**.

The relative importance of these issues will vary from library to library, and indeed within large institutions and systems, but all of them will need to be considered, even if one or more is rejected as irrelevant or inapplicable. The key to preparing a preservation policy is that it must be designed for the library to which it will apply. There are various documents that can be helpful in this context (see Appendix, pp.139–140), but they are no more than guidelines: they are not templates, and certainly not a substitute for proper institutional consideration of the issues.

Preservation administration

The effective administration of a preservation programme depends upon the joint efforts of library management, junior staff and technicians. The role of the manager is essentially in the determination of policy and its supervision, a role that requires a knowledge of the preservation field, without implying any need to acquire its technical skills. This point has often been made, and is now widely accepted in professional circles. Perhaps the one group of exceptions is to be found among some of the more traditional rare book librarians who still seem to regard detailed technical knowledge and even some benchwork skills as an essential part of the librarian's armoury, a view shared to a limited extent by a few educators.

If we leave aside the question of benchwork skills, there are three areas of administrative activity to be considered:

- the **organization of the bindery and other workshops**
- the **determination of the work** to be undertaken and the **styles and techniques** to be employed
- the **role of all staff** in ensuring that materials are handled and used in a way consistent with their optimal survival.

The organization of binderies, photographic studios, conservation laboratories and the like is an integral part of the work of the preservation manager. The first stage, however, is to determine whether it is appropriate to have in-house facilities at all. In 1983–4, 50 out of 332 British libraries that responded to Ratcliffe's survey had an in-house bindery, 26 a conservation workshop, and 86 some kind of repair facilities. A much higher percentage of academic and research libraries had one or more of these facilities than did libraries in any other group. Far more libraries, however, used external facilities; nearly 300 did so for some purpose or other (Ratcliffe, 1984: 17–18). In a larger sample of libraries surveyed ten years later, just over 10% had binderies, and 9% had conservation workshops. Most of these were small: 38 of the 52 binderies and 39 of the 44 workshops had fewer than five staff (Feather, Matthews and Eden 1996: 58). It seems that even libraries with in-house facilities also use external binderies when appropriate. The normal pattern seems to be to use commercial binderies for standard work, such as periodical binding, while undertaking more complex operations in-house. In particular, many libraries prefer to use their own employees and facilities for the repair and conservation of older material, although the British Library has in recent years also used outside binderies for that purpose. Indeed, it has been forcefully argued that there are financial advantages in employing outside organizations or individuals even for high-level conservation work on rare books and manuscripts. There are savings in the indirect costs of employing staff, and it is suggested that the self-employed conservator, working for fees, is likely to maintain a higher rate of productivity than a salaried employee of a library or record office (Banks 1986). On the other hand, it has to be remembered that these conservators can and do charge very high fees indeed, in line with the scarcity of their skills and the demand for their services.

Ultimately, such decisions can be taken only at institutional level. As a general rule, however, it will be the larger academic and research libraries that will have enough work to keep a bindery fully occupied. For other libraries, the use of commercial binding companies is far more cost-effective, especially when, as in most public libraries, the need is for ordinary work such as periodical binding, paperback strengthening and library-style rebinding of damaged books. There has, however, been no really conclusive work on comparative costs (Root 1989). Even in research libraries, however, it is not unusual for 'ordinary' work to be done commercially, while the specialized conservation work, and work on special collections material, is undertaken in-house (Cains 1994). Some commercial firms also undertake what they call 'conservation' work. Although some of the specialist conservators dislike the use of the word in this context, and question the quality of some of the work thus produced, the fact is that the commercial binderies are able to undertake work that is adequate for all normal purposes. They can rebind, reback and make boxes, and some can undertake paper repair. Since these are the key areas of conservation work for all but the most valuable material, these companies are quite satisfactory for almost all purposes. In the last analysis, the decision on whether to establish or maintain an in-house bindery is financial. Where resources are very limited, or the work-flow is comparatively small, there is no real alternative to using outside binderies. In-house facilities are expensive; moreover, there is a limited supply of skilled persons to work in them, and the commercial binderies are, on the whole, able to offer higher wages than are libraries and record offices. The decisions taken by libraries and record offices inevitably and properly have a large financial dimension; the preservation policy, however, should prescribe the quality of the work that external providers will be required to deliver.

The same considerations apply to other preservation facilities. Paper repair and other laboratory activities call for skills that are not widely available, while the facilities themselves occupy a good deal of space. In addition, there are legal requirements in relation to health and safety for the use and storage of chemicals and the use and maintenance of equipment. Traditionally, many record offices have indeed had in-house paper repair and conservation facilities, and continue to do so. In fact, the whole subject of conservation is rightly regarded as a crucial area of the archivist's professional activities and hence an essential part of his or her professional education (Conway 1989). Some research libraries have initiated paper-repair laboratories in recent years, especially for their manuscript collections. Some of these facilities include sophisticated machinery, such as leaf-casters, but the majority of libraries and record offices will continue to look to the commercial sector for the provision of such services. This will be almost universally true of mass deacidification. Although the working plants include a number that are the primary responsibility of national libraries and archives (in Germany, Canada and the United States, for example) (see pp. 117–120), when one of more of the techniques is firmly established as being technically feasible and professionally acceptable, strong commercial interest seems more than likely. This is, after all, an industrial-scale process, and one which can best be provided in an industrial and commercial context.

The case is slightly different with photographic studios. All libraries have some reprographic capacity, if only for photocopying. Most libraries with research collections also have more sophisticated facilities intended to provide transparencies, 35 mm microfilm, bromide prints and the like, for users. These operations usually work on the financial expectation of breaking even, and in some cases as being profit-making. Few in-house studios, however, can cope with large-scale microfilming programmes, although some libraries have established special facilities where surrogate creation has become a principal element in the preservation strategy. The British Library is one such institution (Clements 1988), but few libraries would feel able, financially or technically, to follow that example. Again the problem is one of work-flow. Even for quite large-scale substitution programmes, the commercial microfilm bureaux – or better still micropublishers whose sales will help to offset the cost of creating the master negatives and perhaps produce a royalty or fee for the library – are a distinctly preferable option.

Digitization is not yet fully operational as a preservation technique (see pp. 72–75), although its technical feasibility is now well-established. Any institution that does eventually embark on a large-scale digitization programme will need to decide whether it is cost-effective to maintain its own facilities. In universities, the likelihood is that such work will be undertaken jointly with computing services departments, although increasingly libraries and computing services are coming together administratively just as they are converging technologically. It can also be expected, however, that there will be continued commercial interest in digitization, as there has been in the production and publication of microforms, and indeed in the creation of optical discs containing text and data archives.

Whether the work is undertaken in-house or externally, it will be library staff who determine what work is actually to be done. This decision-making process falls essentially into two stages: first, the material to be repaired has to be selected, a subject with which we have already dealt at some length (see pp. 91–95); secondly, the nature of the work to be undertaken has to be decided, and for this to be done effectively some technical knowledge is indeed essential, so that the librarian understands the available options.

Having decided in principle that a particular item or a particular class of material is to be preserved, the next stage is to decide whether preservation is to be in original format or in surrogate form. Normally, it will be the original format that needs repair. The preservation policy will determine what may be done, although, according to the circumstances, a greater or lesser degree of professional judgement may also be needed. Some cases are very straightforward: a book in heavy use will have to be rebound or repaired to ensure that it stands up to the demands made on it, unless a replacement can be obtained. Others are more complicated: a book from special collections with detached boards can be tied, boxed or rebacked, and which course of action is chosen will depend on estimates of cost, usage and importance. Individual decisions are vitally important; it is equally important, however, that they are consistent with each other and with the policy of the library as a whole. That is why a prescriptive preservation policy is the key to success.

Surrogate creation is, in general, very uneconomic for single items such as one book or a small group of documents. The larger the number of uniform items, such as a run of a newspaper, the more economically attractive does surrogacy become, especially if there might be a spin-off in the sale of copies of the microfilm to other libraries. In 1986, it was calculated that the cost of a 35 mm microfilm of a 300-page book was very slightly more than the cost of a made-to-measure box for the same book, and less than one-third of the price of a full-scale rebinding. The figures were £19.50, £18.72 and £67.08 respectively (Wilson 1988: 20) On this basis, preservation by microfilming might be argued to make sound economic sense even for individual items, but in practice this is rarely true.

It is not usual in Britain, although it is in some American libraries, to discard the originals once the master negative has been made. If the book is important enough to film, it is important enough to need more than mere neglect to preserve the original. Hence, in addition to the cost of filming, there will also be the cost of the box, and perhaps even of significant (and hence expensive) repairs or rebinding. Preservation microfilming generally makes sense only when undertaken on a large scale for a large number of items; this is why a run of a newspaper is so ideal a candidate for such treatment. When programmes are undertaken cooperatively or as joint ventures with publishers, the costs may be even more favourable to the library (McClung 1986).

At present, microform is the only truly working technique for the creation of document surrogates, although digitization is certainly very close to implementation as a tool of mass preservation (see pp. 72–75). The costs of digitization are, however, high; the calculations that have been made are inevitably theoretical at this stage, and generally compare the cost of digital archiving with the cost of preserving documents in a deposit library (Commission on Preservation and Access 1995: 30–5). In the longer term, however, it is likely that the costs of digital storage will decrease until they compare very favourably with those of storing traditional formats. The digitization option will then become one that is very seriously considered for large collections of documents which would be expensive to repair or to store.

All preservation and conservation work is expensive, whether it uses the thousand-year-old skills of the bookbinder or the high technology of digitization. It remains the case that preservation costs can be reduced significantly only if materials are properly stored and used in the first place to minimize the problems which we will bequeath to our successors. In practice, one course of action, or rather inaction, that is widely adopted is what has sometimes been called benign neglect, that is storage in reasonably good conditions together with the enforcement of high standards of handling and use. For rarely used materials this has been a favoured option in some libraries in recent years, not least because it has the great merit of costing almost nothing. More recently, however, the practice has been challenged from an authoritative source (Enright, Hellinga and Leigh 1989: 36); the argument turns essentially on the need to define *why* material is to be preserved, and by whom it will be accessed and used. These are issues needing consideration at national rather than institutional level (see pp. 156–157).

Whatever work is to be carried out, it is essential that the binder (or other technical worker) has clear instructions from the librarian or archivist (Henderson 1987). The binder will carry out such instructions, but cannot be expected to interpret them or make deductions about them. It is certainly not the binder's business to guess at what they ought to have been when they are either absent or inadequate. For straightforward work, only straightforward instructions are required. These should specify the general nature of the work to be done, the materials to be used and any special requirements. Thus, for rebinding a recent book, the specification need be no more than 'library binding, blue cloth', together with a note of the words or any other matter (such as a shelf-mark), if any, to be embossed on the spine. For periodicals, the instructions are typically a little more complicated, since they have to specify how the parts are to be arranged, whether such material as covers, advertising pages and supplements are to be retained, and if so where they are to be bound in. The instructions will also specify what is to be done about the title-page, index and table of contents, as well as external matters such as the colour of cloth to be used and the wording on the spine. The last two items will be standardized in most libraries, but they do differ from library to library. Many libraries keep standard or specimen bindings in their own binderies which are then imitated year after year to maintain uniformity on the shelves. Commercial binderies have their own specimens, standards and exemplars from which the customer can choose, but they will also create and maintain a design to the customer's own specification. Instructions are normally sent to the bindery in writing, and often on order forms designed for the purpose. In some libraries the binding records are now automated, and instructions therefore appear in the form of hard-copy printout from the relevant file. Finally, when completed work is returned from the binder, at least a random sample is normally checked to ensure that the instructions have indeed been followed.

Preservation, however, is not a matter for specialists alone, or indeed only for professional librarians. It is the concern of all staff and *all users* of a library. A great deal can be achieved in a preservation programme by creating the conditions in which the rate of deterioration of materials is reduced to a minimum. This can, of course, be very expensive if it is conceived in terms of environmental control systems, significant building modifications, and the like. It can be done very cheaply, however, by simple housekeeping measures that are an integral part of the administration of a well-run library. Junior staff are the key to success. It is they who handle books and deal with users. They can act both as the detectors of the first signs of damage or decay, and as the exemplars in the handling and care of materials.

Good housekeeping begins with the shelves. Ideally, these should be of metal, not wood, since metal is not susceptible to the biological hazards that can beset any organic substance. It is also easier to keep clean, and less likely to be broken or damaged. The proper care of books on the shelves is the starting-point of a preservation programme. This means, among other things, regular and careful dusting using soft dusters and no chemical cleaning medium. Even in heavily used reference collections, most books spend most of their lives on the shelves. Junior staff have to be taught to keep the shelves tidy, and in particular to ensure that they are always tidy at the beginning of the day. This has the psychological effect on users of encouraging them to try to maintain that level of tidiness, whereas untidy shelves can only worsen through the day.

A few simple rules also need to be applied by the professional staff in determining where and how books shall be stored. Outsize books should be shelved upright in a separate sequence, not foredge-down in normally spaced shelves. Very large volumes, such as atlases or bound volumes of newspapers, should be shelved flat, even in open-access areas. Special shelving, or other storage systems, is needed for maps and audiovisual materials. Current parts of periodicals may need protective covers as a temporary measure before they go for boxing or binding. Pamphlets, again in a special sequence, are better stored in boxes than directly on the shelves. These are all examples of good practice, and are not beyond the realistic aspirations and capability of any library.

Staff and users alike should be exhorted to look after books. Staff should be encouraged not to overload trolleys, not to carry too many books, not to pile books too high on desks and tables or on or behind counters. Trolleys are needed for books returned to the circulation desk before they go for sorting and shelving. The trolleys should also be kept tidy, and, when they are moved, moved carefully. In all of these cases, exhortation is probably more effective than instruction, but it is also important that the professional staff make clear to juniors the extent and the limits of their authority in dealing with any recalcitrant users, and are then prepared to support them.

Staff in general need to be made aware that preservation is an aspect of collection management; otherwise some of this may seem a little trivial or pedantic. In particular, circulation staff should be empowered, and indeed required, to set aside books returned from loan in need of repair. This is not for the purpose of punishing a particular user who may or may not have been responsible for the damage. It is rather because a minor and cheap repair now may save the time and expense of a major repair later. A culture in which prevention is better than cure is created by example, and it is the responsibility of all professional staff to assist in its creation. In older buildings, all staff need to be alert for the first signs of serious biological events such as fungal growths, moulds and damp patches. A proper reporting system will be needed to ensure that any such suspicions reach the preservation manager, or other responsible professional, immediately.

Building design, the internal layout of the building and furnishings are also critical elements in preservation. In research libraries, or in rare book rooms, it is essential that readers' tables are sufficiently generous in size to allow books to be used properly without piling them one on top of another. Where particularly valuable or fragile books and manuscripts are being used, table-top lecterns are essential; plastic forceps to hold the page open without exerting too much pressure on it are a useful additional precaution.

Some regulations are also necessary to ensure effective preservation. Apart from obvious rules about the use and misuse of books, it is normal to forbid the use of flat-platen photocopying machines with older books or manuscripts. Books in special collections are not normally available for circulation and are rarely loaned to other libraries, unless for exhibition under carefully regulated conditions. Although many of these considerations and regulations apply principally to older and more valuable materials, the general philosophy of concern and care they imply can usefully be transferred to the general maintenance of the library's stock.

None of this will happen by itself. A library that wishes to create a preservation-conscious culture needs a senior member of staff responsible for it. In many, and perhaps most, libraries this is not a full-time job, and is perhaps most logically associated either with the post-holder responsible for collection management and development, or with the professional librarian with overall responsibility for the running of the building. The essential function of the preservation manager is that he or she has a general oversight of all the matters we have been discussing, and is, therefore, in a position to have a policy-level view of the library's preservation situation. He or she is the determiner of the policies and priorities that will in turn allow logical and consistent decisions to be made on individual cases. The preservation manager also has some specific responsibilities. One, of great importance, is the compilation of the disaster control plan. In some large academic and research libraries, and in most major record offices and archives, the post of preservation manager, under whatever title, is now a full-time senior position. Indeed, those libraries that have made most progress towards defining and solving their preservation problems have been those prepared to invest in professional as well as technical personnel, so that long-term policies can be evolved and their implementation properly monitored.

The senior binders are among the most important advisers to the preservation manager, especially where the repair of older material is concerned. The final decisions are, of course, taken by the librarian, but it is important to recognize that the binder has his or her own expertise, and it should be exploited to the full. In particular, an experienced binder has a wide-ranging knowledge of materials and techniques which few, if any, professional librarians can equal. A binder is an implementer rather than an originator of policy, but typically has a fairly free hand within the broad outlines of institutional policies. The senior binder also has to take on a managerial and administrative role in his or her own right, being in day-to-day charge of the bindery, and reporting to the preservation manager. This may be a fairly substantial task, although it should not be allowed to divert the binder too much from the regular work of the bindery. In a typical library bindery, operating on a modest scale, there will be one or two fully trained binders, and perhaps an apprentice. One of these people, usually the senior, may reserve for personal attention the exceptionally skilled tasks of finishing and decorating, especially in leather. Collating and sewing, regarded as less skilled and more functional work, are also usually separated out. The preservation manager also needs clerical support for the maintenance of records of work sent to the bindery and to outside companies, and for the general administration of the department. Administrative support becomes even more important if the manager is also responsible for a conservation laboratory, with one or two paper repairers and perhaps other scientists and technicians, or a photographic studio, with camera operators, film processors and clerical assistance. The preservation brief, conceived in its broadest terms, covers so many aspects of the library's activities that it inevitably comes to occupy a major place among staff commitments.

Training for preservation

Preservation, in its broadest sense as an aspect of collection management, and orientated towards the provision of access for users, is a comparatively new element in librarianship, although it derives from many much older areas of activity and draws on long-established expertise. The present generation of preservation managers have generally come from one of two sources, with a few crucial exceptions. They were either conservators and bookbinders, or rare book librarians. It is clear that neither gives the ideal background or training for preservation as it is now practised. Until very recently, however, the library and information science schools have either neglected preservation altogether or have, like some libraries, marginalized it into such fields as rare book librarianship or archive studies. There is some evidence of improvement in this, and in the UK there has certainly been a growing awareness of the importance of the subject among educators since the low point recorded in the early 1980s (Cloonan 1994). By contrast, preservation has always been central to archives education; it is now recognized as having a managerial as well as a technical dimension (Forde 1987). Curriculum recommendations for both archives and librarianship students have recently been published, and will, it is hoped, influence developments in the next few years (Cook 1982; Feather 1990).

There have also been some attempts to develop professional education programmes for preservation managers. The first and most successful of these was initiated at the School of Library Service at Columbia University, New York, in 1980. When that School closed, the programme was transferred to the University of Texas at Austin where it still flourishes. No similar programme exists in Europe, although some of the European library and information science departments do teach preservation management to generalists, and there is some interest in establishing a specialized programme (Federici 1995).

An even more complex issue is that of training non-professional staff. In both the USA and the UK, the training of non-professional staff (now more properly called paraprofessionals) has always been quite distinct from professional education, and held at arms' length by both the professional associations and the library and information science departments. This is breaking down in a limited way; for example, at Rutgers University in the USA a Professional Development Certificate Program in Preservation is not confined to professional librarians (Swartzburg 1995a). For the most part, however, the responsibility for the training of paraprofessionals remains where it has always been: with their employers, where practice varies from the excellent to the execrable (Feather 1995). Moreover, it is only very recently that suitable training materials have been produced to help trainers who themselves may be far from expert in the field (National Preservation Office 1994).

While it is essential that librarians are aware of preservation as a management issue in their institutions, no work can actually be carried out unless the relevant skills are available. We have already discussed the relative merits of in-house and external binderies, and referred to the salary differentials which often seem to exist between the two. In either case, however, trained personnel are essential. In the early 1980s, there was alleged to be a skill shortage, especially in craft binding techniques, although it was said that the position was not as bad in the UK as in the USA (Stam 1983: 3). Recent research, however, suggest that there is now a rather closer correlation between the numbers of skilled workers and of available jobs (Feather, Matthews and Eden 1996: 68-72).

The situation with regard to the training of binders, technicians and other benchworkers is somewhat confused. In the early 1980s there were about 20 courses in Britain that appeared to be giving training in binding skills that were relevant to library and archive conservation, but in the absence of any central validating body it is difficult to know what standards these courses attained. It seems, however, that their diplomates satisfy all but the most exacting needs for all but the most specialized work. The Society of Archivists has responded to the needs of record offices by devising its own training schemes which have achieved a deservedly high reputation (Thomas 1984).

If there is a problem, there is no easy solution to it. Bookbinding is not a prestigious occupation, and it is not well paid. Commercial binderies will continue to be the main source of newly trained personnel, and it is perhaps inevitable that those companies will come to be even more dominant in library binding in Britain.

Conclusion

The management of a successful preservation programme is a joint venture between the librarian or archivist and the technician. But a great deal can be achieved without ever going near a bench or a studio. A properly managed library is one in which the information resource is properly protected, not so that it becomes a museum, but so that it can be used. Use, however, has a context, and part of the context is the wider provision of library and information services. No library stands alone: modern technology has given us greater and wider access than ever before, and it is in that context that preservation policy has to be understood. This chapter has been firmly focused on individual institutions. In the next, and final, chapter, we shall turn to the national and indeed international context in which preservation and access policies can only be fully understood and fully exploited.

Appendix: Guidelines on preservation policies

This is a selective list of some of the published documents that can be helpful in developing a preservation policy. It is emphasized, however, that they are only guidelines (see p. 126), and that institutions will ultimately need to take their own decisions. A more detailed analysis of these and other documents will be found in Feather, Matthews and Eden (1996: 97-107).

Chapman, Patricia. *Guidelines on preservation and conservation policies in libraries and archives.* Paris: UNESCO (PGI-90/WS/7), 1990.
This was based on a survey undertaken for UNESCO in 1985–6 (Clements 1986b). It is a valuable general guide for those who are developing a policy for the preservation and use of conventional materials.

Dureau, J-M, and Clements, D. W. G. *Principles for the preservation and conservation of library materials.* The Hague: IFLA (IFLA Professional Reports, 8), 1986.
The *IFLA Principles*, as this has become commonly known, is from the same intellectual and professional stable as the UNESCO document. It represent a broadly based international consensus, but predates the recognition of issues relating to electronic data. A revised version is currently being developed by the IFLA Preservation and Conservation Core Programme and the Section on Conservation.

National Preservation Office. *Preservation guidelines.* London: The British Library, 1991.
This invaluable leaflet gives practical assistance to any librarian seeking to put a policy in place.

Library and Information Service Council (Wales)/LISC (Cymru). *Conservation guidelines. Survey and action./Canllawiau Cadwraeth. Arolwg a gweithredu.* Aberystwyth: National Library of Wales/Llyfrgell Genedlaethol Cymru, 1993.
A similarly short, practical document, intended for librarians (and, to a lesser extent, archivists) who seek assistance in putting together a preservation policy.

Chapter 7
THE PROFESSIONAL CONTEXT: PRESERVATION AND ACCESS

Introduction

The design and implementation of a preservation policy does not take place only at institutional level. It is sustained by regional, national and international policies and services. These reflect, in turn, the growing professional commitment that is found in the activities of national libraries, professional associations, governments and international organizations. This professional context has provided the essential background against which local developments have taken place over the last decade of intensified activity. It has significantly assisted those librarians who have been concerned with preservation in demonstrating to colleagues and paymasters alike the seriousness with which the profession as a whole has approached the issue.

As we have seen, the current concern with preservation really developed out of two immediate causes, one general – the growing awareness, in the 1960s, of the rapid deterioration of embrittled books and documents, especially in American libraries – and the other specific – the Florence flood of 1966, which forced librarians to recognize the need to sustain the traditional skills of book restoration and repair. Of course, many librarians and all archivists had retained their interest in preservation, although it was perhaps seen largely as a matter for those principally concerned with older materials in research libraries. It was rarely if ever linked to wider questions of collection management or to other and even broader professional concerns about access to information and information media.

That link can no longer be ignored. New technologies themselves force us to recognize the critical nature of the decisions we have to take about what to preserve and how to preserve it, and how information is be made fully accessible. There are also, however, key strategic concerns which make it essential to re-examine the issues. Partly because of technological innovation, but partly also for political and financial reasons, libraries are operating in a very different world from the 1960s. The negative dimension of this is that the age of expansion is over, probably for ever. The positive side has been the need to find imaginative solutions to problems old and new. Technology has offered at least some of these solutions by breaking down finally and for ever the idea that a library can be self-sufficient and independent. Shared information resources and the far wider availability of information mean that we can reconsider our approach to the preservation of materials and data. Information technology can, to some extent, overcome the problems created by financial constraints. More than at any time in the past, the relationship between preservation and access can be clearly seen.

The purpose of this final chapter is to trace that process of change, not as a simple historical investigation, but rather to show the broad context within which preservation and collection management are properly placed. Both the recognition of the embrittlement problem and the Florence flood had the incidental effect of forcing librarians to think about the cooperative and international aspects of preservation. National libraries took a vital role in developing new techniques. As we have seen, many of the deacidification processes, for example, were initially developed with funding from national institutions; the involvement of the private sector was with a view to providing central facilities that would be available to many different libraries and archives (see pp. 117–118). The same was true of much development work in other fields. The Library of Congress, for example, sponsored important pioneering work on the application of optical disc technology to preservation (Welsh 1986). Now that CD-ROM has become one of the most familiar of digital information carriers, we can see how this work has borne fruit. Indeed, the Library of Congress has consistently seen its work on deacidification, optical disc technology, and, most recently, digitization, as being part of a contribution to solving the global preservation problem, and it has strongly supported international efforts to put preservation on the professional agenda (Welsh 1987).

Cooperative efforts towards preservation in the 1980s usually took the form of large-scale cooperative microfilming programmes. They were widely commended in theory, and although there were inevitable problems in implementing some individual projects, there were also some notable successes (see pp. 121–122). The cost and scale of major surrogate creation programmes, like that of the development of new preservation technologies, was so large that only groups of institutions, with major financial backers, could undertake them. Indeed, the extent of the preservation problem, and the cost of the solutions to it, would have forced libraries to cooperate, even if they had not been willing to do so. Above all, however, cooperative information preservation came to be understood as the key to access and use, the twin lodestones of modern librarianship. In a remarkable and far-sighted paper published in 1982, the then Director-General of the British Library Reference Division argued that preservation and access, far from being in conflict, were inextricably linked, for access is not possible if information is not preserved (Wilson 1982). In the early 1980s, that might have been understood rather differently from our understanding more than a decade later, but the principle remains unchanged. We simply have more powerful tools at our command.

However powerful our technologies might become, we cannot neglect the basic physical facts. For so long as books and journals are published on paper, we shall need to preserve them or their contents in some form. At the same time, we need to make judgments about what exactly we do need to preserve, and in how many copies. Cooperative collection development projects, with their wide implications for resource sharing and library funding arrangements, were also thought to be an important element in this equation in the 1970s and 1980s (Stam 1986; Battin 1989). This is still the case, but increasingly it is expressed rather differently as the need to think in terms of cooperation in retention policies, with access provided either by document delivery services or by networked access to digitized data. The Australian concept of the 'disseminated national collection' is an interesting model, embodying as it does the idea that a national collection is not to be seen simply as the contents of the national library, but as comprehending all the nationally important holdings of many libraries.

If the current interest in preservation as a tool of information management can be argued to have begun in the USA, there is no doubt that it has been enthusiastically received elsewhere in the world. It is perhaps helpful to begin by tracing recent developments and initiatives in the UK to illustrate the increasing pervasiveness of the issue and the general directions of development that are being evolved.

The British experience

Throughout the 1970s leading librarians in Britain, many of whom were in frequent and close contact with their opposite numbers in the USA, became increasingly aware of the preservation problem. As we have seen (see pp. 11–12), it was made a major priority in the Reference Division of the newly created British Library. At the same time, other major institutions, such as the Bodleian Library, Oxford, reorientated their traditional binding and repair activities towards a more coordinated conservation programme (Turner 1984). All libraries that were concerned for the permanent retention of the greater part of their stocks began to recognize the need for active intervention to facilitate this, and to initiate appropriate programmes (Price 1987).

The British Library was consistently the leader in this field of professional endeavour. As well as taking steps towards attacking its own preservation problems, it also helped to facilitate the development of national policies. In 1980 the Library's Research and Development Department (BLRDD) commissioned F. W. Ratcliffe, then Librarian of Cambridge University, to conduct an investigation of preservation policies and practices in the UK (Ratcliffe 1984). This was to be quite unlike the preservation surveys that were by that time a fairly common feature of the library scene in the USA. Ratcliffe was principally concerned to gather information about facilities, personnel, training and attitudes rather than about books and documents. Indeed, a simultaneous investigation by

David H. Stam, at that time Director of the Research Collections at New York Public Library, was also funded by BLRDD; Stam showed how different were British and American preservation problems and professional perceptions (Stam 1983).

The Ratcliffe and Stam reports provided a framework upon which national policies could be built. Although their approaches were in some ways quite different, they agreed in many of their conclusions: both emphasized the need for the raising of professional and public awareness about the preservation issue; both advocated greater national and international cooperation; both pointed out the necessity of education and training for both professional and technical staff. Many of these ideas bore fruit and, in particular, the concept of 'awareness raising' became central to the British response to the preservation issue. The middle 1980s were difficult times for public-sector institutions in Britain. Large-scale new initiatives could be funded only by either diverting diminishing resources from existing activities, or by raising money in the private sector or from charitable foundations. All of these methods came to be used in due course, but the first step was clearly the need to establish a proper perception of the importance of preservation. The publication of the Ratcliffe Report was in itself a significant move in that direction.

Even more important was the almost immediate adoption of one of Ratcliffe's key recommendations, the establishment of what he called a 'national advisory and research centre' (Ratcliffe 1984: 36–8). This idea was realized in late 1984, within months of the publication of the Ratcliffe Report, by the establishment by the British Library of the National Preservation Office (NPO), which has come to play a central strategic role in library preservation in the UK. Its role is partly advisory, both in helping smaller libraries with their preservation problems and in giving policy advice at every level, and partly educational, supporting conferences and promotional activities of various kinds (Clements 1986a). The National Preservation Advisory Committee (NPAC), which works with it, links NPO into the profession at large by a complex structure of representation from all sectors of librarianship, as well as from the archives field and from professional associations and organizations. NPAC's subsidiary panels, one of conservators and one of educators, carried its work forward into two areas of particular concern – skill training and professional education.

The need to raise awareness among British librarians and funding bodies has been reflected in many NPO activities. A series of seminars, beginning in 1986, brought together 40 or 50 of the most committed librarians, archivists and educators on a regular basis. It has also provided the papers for a series of useful publications in a field in which up-to-date British literature was in short supply. With financial support either from the Preservation Service or from the Research and Development Department, the NPO has also been involved in projects on disaster preparedness planning (Tregarthen Jenkin 1987), curriculum development (Feather and Lusher 1988) and scientific work on strengthening embrittled paper (King 1986, 1989). It became the editorial office for *Library conservation news,* an invaluable source of information about the preservation field in the UK. Private-sector support has provided the funding for annual prizes for the best conservation project in a British library (National Preservation Office 1989). It has published leaflets and bibliographies, made data available through the British Library's online information services (and subsequently on its Website, Portico – <URL: http://portico.bl.uk:70/0/portico/services/preserv/npo-quick.txt>) and acted as a clearing house for information on techniques, materials, suppliers and personnel. In the early 1990s, it has focused on security (Burrows and Cooper 1992), microfilming (National Preservation Office 1993), and training (National Preservation Office 1994). Its current activities are detailed on its Web pages.

Neither the NPO nor indeed the British Library itself has a directive role, but both can exert great influence. The increased awareness of preservation needs has led to greater emphasis on preservation in professional practice. In turn, this has also made it possible to raise funding for specific projects. The Wolfson Foundation, for example, has donated substantial funds, administered by the British Library, for preservation work in smaller collections throughout the country (Awards 1989). The $3m donation from the Mellon Foundation for preservation microfilming and associated activities has also been handled by the NPO (see p. 122), as has the fund established by the government in 1989 for the conservation and repair of manuscripts. More recently, the NPO has been consulted on grants made out of funds derived from the National Lottery.

This account of British Library and NPO activities in preservation – all, it should be remembered, in addition to the Library's very considerable in-house programmes – is by no means exhaustive, for important new initiatives are coming on-stream all the time. It is, however, enough to give some idea of the range and depth of the British Library's involvement, and its interpretation of its national leadership role. Most major libraries in Britain now take preservation very seriously indeed, and many that cannot afford extensive activities have recognized the need for them.

At the same time, there is growing evidence for an increased sophistication of understanding of the issues involved. The rather strident tones in which enthusiasts presented the case for preservation in the mid-1980s perhaps sometimes disguised the real significance of their message for libraries. Universal preservation of everything was never the objective, and yet it sometimes seemed that it was. As a result, some librarians simply dismissed the relevance of preservation to their concerns; one public library director dismissed it (at an NPO seminar!) as being, in essence, nothing to do with him (Liddle 1988). By 1993–4, however, there was evidence of widespread understanding of the issues, and a recognition of the need for selectivity. In essence, public libraries identified preservation with their special collections (especially their local studies collections), just as many university libraries did (Eden, Feather and Matthews 1993; 1994). There is substantial evidence that, despite financial constraints and many other calls on limited funding, preservation is given appropriate priority in many institutions. As we have already suggested, that priority is indeed institutionally determined (see pp. 91–96).

European experiences: France, Germany and elsewhere

The development of national policies inevitably mirrors both national cultural preoccupations and national political structures. Thus, the British Library must lead by example and exhortation, and in recent years has had to seek external funding for many activities as well as look to generating income from some of its operations. In some countries, however, the national library or its sponsoring ministry can enforce policy on the nation's library system as a whole. Governments even pay for implementation. In France, for example, the Bibliothèque Nationale de France itself has to some extent taken the lead by establishing its own *Centre de conservation* at Sablé, but the ministries responsible for libraries have also played key roles. As a consequence, France was considered by one knowledgeable and astute commentator to have the most systematic library preservation programme among all the member states of the European Community by the late 1980s (Wilson 1988). The Bibliothèque Nationale had established its own *Plan de sauvegarde* in 1979. This followed on from the report of the Caillet Commission, which had, in effect, conducted a massive preservation survey of the library's holdings. The government provided an annual budget of no less than Ff10m from 1980 onwards to implement the plan. This included the establishment of new studios and workshops, the initiation of huge microfilming and repair programmes, and support for research and development work on deacidification. In France, as elsewhere, the scale of need far outstretches the scale of provision, and even the exceptional generosity of the French government is inadequate to meet the massive needs of the Bibliothèque Nationale. In the last five years, the building of the new national library has been the occasion for further refinement of preservation policies (Oddos 1991).

Nationally, French policies evolved from the report of the Desgraves Commission in 1982, substantially adopted in 1984 (Ministère de la culture 1982). This report, sponsored by the Direction du livre et de la lecture in the Ministry of Culture, was particularly concerned with the widespread preservation problems to be found in France's historic public libraries, the *bibliothèques municipales*. Unlike most of their British and American counterparts, the French public libraries have large and important holdings of old and rare material, much of it derived from the pre-Revolutionary private and ecclesiastical libraries which formed their foundation collections at the turn of the 18th and 19th centuries, when they were confiscated from their former owners. The Desgraves report recommended a wide range of measures, including the establishment of regional centres for conservation and microfilming work; better provision for the exploitation of collections through the creation and dissemination of guides, inventories and catalogues; and programmes of education and training for professional and technical staff and of awareness-raising for users and the general public. Some of this has been effected; regional centres exist, a union catalogue of microfilmed newspapers was published in 1988, and there has been a good deal of educational activity.

Just as the French experience reflects the strong centrifugal tendencies of the French state (at least until the middle 1980s), so the recent history of preservation in Germany reflects the strength of that country's regional structures. There is no single national library, but there are very important regional research libraries. Reflecting, no doubt, the important historical role of the scholar-librarian in German culture, a scholar rather than a librarian was commissioned to undertake the national preservation survey in the former West Germany, although it should be added that he was also a distinguished student of the history of books and libraries. Not surprisingly, he produced a report that reflected both his own humanistic interests and his long-standing knowledge of the British Library and of British and American traditions of bibliographical scholarship (Fabian 1983). In the follow-up to the Fabian Report, a working group of the Deutsche Forschungsgemeinschaft, which coordinates interregional resource sharing among the West German libraries, produced a number of specific recommendations. Most of these were concerned with access to materials and with union cataloguing rather than with preservation *per se,* although one recommendation did deal with the need for central conservation facilities for the treatment of important historical materials (Kaltwasser 1986). Reunification brought its own problems, but it also made more widely available some of the technologies that had been developed at the Deutches Bucherie in Leipzig, which was a Regional Centre for IFLA's Core Programme in Preservation and Conservation (see pp. 153–154).

Many other European countries, both east and west, have undertaken preservation surveys; some have subsequently initiated programmes to act on the results. There are many common problems in terms of underfunding, neglect of collections, unsuitable buildings and lack of conservation facilities and expertise, as well as failure on the part of officials, librarians and users to understand the urgency and seriousness of the problem. This was well documented for western Europe in the 1980s (Clements and Arnoult 1988); only now, in this as in other matters, is the full state of affairs in the former Soviet Union and the other former socialist countries becoming apparent.

Within the European Union, there has been much effective support for library cooperation. Wilson's survey of 1986–7 has already been cited several times (Wilson 1988); it is an invaluable account of the situation in the member states at a time when the major EC [as it then was] library initiatives were in the planning stage. Wilson was particularly concerned with information technology applications in preservation, but he interpreted his brief widely enough to be able to include scientific developments such as deacidification research and the use of photographic and digitized surrogate media for information preservation. Little truly interstate collaboration was revealed, but he suggested a number of areas in which it might be developed. These included support for interstate catalogues, the funding of relevant research and development and the encouragement of educational initiatives. It was out of one of his recommendations that the European Register of Microform Masters was eventually to grow (Feather and Vitiello 1991). There are other European initiatives outside the immediate auspices of the European Union; at the time of writing, the Ligue de Bibliothèques Européenes de Recherche (LIBER) is sponsoring a survey of preservation policies in all its member libraries, which cover the whole continent including the EU member states, other western and central European countries, and Russia and the former Soviet bloc countries in Europe. Finally, a European Commission on Preservation and Access was established in 1994; it has no formal official status, but brings together scholars and preservation specialists from several countries, seeks to promote cooperative work and hopes to act as a lobbyist for preservation at European level (European Commission on Preservation and Access 1996).

Beyond Europe: the USA and Australia

For historical, cultural and political reasons, the approaches adopted to address preservation issues in the USA and in Australia have been different from those that have developed in Europe, as well as, of course, being different from each other. While this is not the place for a comprehensive study of preservation policies in either country, it is useful to consider their experiences, for both the problems and the solutions are very relevant to many aspects of the British and European situation.

As we have seen, one of the key problems of modern library preservation – the embrittlement of acidic paper – was first identified in the USA, and strategies to combat it first began to be developed there (see pp. 4–7). While embrittlement was certainly not a uniquely American problem, it was more predominant than in Europe, and has continued to be a major concern. The idea of a *national* preservation policy became a subject of discussion in the USA in the 1970s, largely in the wake of the establishment of the Preservation Office in the Library of Congress. Indeed, the Library of Congress was seen by some, not least its own staff, as a key player in national developments (Poole 1976). There were, however, other initiatives, of which one of the most important was taken by the Association of Research Libraries (ARL), which had made detailed proposals for a national preservation policy (Haas 1972). There were, however, many obstacles to the development of national policies in a federal nation with no single national library, and only slowly were the major players identified. Indeed, one of the most important early developments was the establishment of the New England [now Northeast] Document Conservation Center in 1973, a shared facility for the benefit of smaller libraries that could not afford to develop their own workshops and binderies; there was some federal funding, but the initiative had come from the state librarians of the six New England states (O'Connell 1994). In the evolution of nationwide activities, the Library of Congress and the Research Libraries Group (RLG), founded in 1974, were critical catalysts; it was, however, the Commission on Preservation and Access, founded in 1986 after five years of preliminary work by the Council on Library Resources, and the injection of funds from the National Endowment for the Humanities (NEH) that gave the real impetus for action at this level (Battin 1989; Stam 1991).

There was a general recognition that the preservation problem was too large for any one institution to address by itself. As important, however, was the realization that preservation and access were indissolubly linked; this was indeed symbolized in the name of the Commission on Preservation and Access, a title adopted by its aspirant European counterpart. National policies in the United States have been largely built around coordinated programmes of mass microfilming of embrittled materials, with coordination through the distribution of NEH funding for this purpose. An example will illustrate the point: at Columbia University, New York, the NEH has funded a three-year microfilming programme of library materials on the history of economic thought in the last 150 years, which is both a part of Columbia's own programme for dealing with its vast holdings of embrittled material and part of a coordinated strategy to avoid duplication in the creation of surrogates (Columbia University 1996). At the same time ARL continues to play an important role, through the provision of resource guides and other support services for its member libraries (Association of Research Libraries 1996). A review of the work of the Commission on Preservation and Access, while by no means complacent, suggested that it had met many of its initial objectives, and recommended the broadening of its brief which, during the 1990s, has led it to engage successfully on such issues as digitization and the preservation of digitized data, as well as to be more prominent on the international stage (Commission on Preservation and Access 1991).

In Australia, as in Britain and the USA, preservation became a live issue during the 1980s, with a preservation committee being created in 1986 by the Australian Council of Libraries and Information Services, leading to the establishment in 1992 of a National Preservation Office in the National Library (Lyall 1994: 272–3). The establishment of this Office, as a national focal point for preservation activities, had been recommended in a report published in 1989 which effectively set the agenda for library preservation in the country (Lyall and Schmidt 1989). The role of the Australian NPO is to take a national overview of preservation needs and policies, and above all to lead the drive towards the development of national retention policies which, as in the UK, is coming to be seen as a vital strategy for the future. The Office, however, is concerned with the whole spectrum of preservation and conservation from the treatment of original materials to electronic preservation (National Preservation Office 1996).

The world stage: IFLA and UNESCO

Even the very cursory accounts in the last few pages have revealed the extent of a common agenda for preservation across many countries. This is no accident, for this has been a field in which international cross-fertilization of ideas has been conspicuous and valuable. IFLA has played a critical role in promoting the preservation issue and in facilitating international cooperation and exchange of ideas. A Core Programme in Preservation and Conservation (PAC) was established in 1984, and has been active ever since. PAC was originally based at the Library of Congress, but responsibility has now been assumed by the Bibliothèque nationale de France. PAC has a number of regional centres around the world whose purpose is to act as referral agencies, information disseminators and trainers for both professionals and technicians from the countries of their respective regions. At present there are PAC centres established at Leipzig in Germany (for eastern Europe), at the Library of Congress (for North America), at Caracas in Venezuela (for Latin America), at the National Diet Library in Tokyo (for east Asia) and at the National Library of Australia (for Australasia). Education, training and awareness-raising lie at the heart of PAC's mission. The formal launch of the programme took place at a meeting of the Conference of Directors of National Libraries held in Vienna in 1986. This meeting, jointly sponsored by IFLA and UNESCO, took as one of its themes the need for education and training for preservation (Smith 1987). Training seminars for librarians and conservators from eastern Europe were held at Leipzig (in 1986), for those from francophone Africa at Sablé (in 1989) and for anglophone African library and archive directors in London and Loughborough in the UK in 1990. A seminar in Nairobi was particularly valuable in bringing current ideas on preservation to the African continent itself (Arnoult, Kremp and Musembi 1995).

This does not complete the list of PAC's activities, many of which have been undertaken in collaboration with IFLA's Section on Conservation. Perhaps the most important to reach fruition so far is the compilation of guidelines on conservation edited by David Clements and Jeanne-Marie Dureau (Clements and Dureau 1986) (see also p. 140), a document intended to help librarians to begin their preservation planning and policy-making. Projects in progress include a revision of this document, work on the preservation of photographic collections, the planning of a conference on the economic implications of preservation programmes and the development of a model preservation survey report (Varlamoff 1995).

UNESCO has been active in the field of library preservation in several respects. In a sense, this brings us full circle, for it was UNESCO that coordinated the rescue efforts at Florence, which some now see as the beginning of the revival of interest in conservation and preservation. Increasingly, however, preservation has come to be seen in UNESCO, as elsewhere, as an aspect of information service provision rather than being solely a matter of cultural heritage. Many of UNESCO's most important recent initiatives in the library preservation field have been under the auspices of the Programme Générale d'Information (PGI). In particular, the Records and Archives Management Programme (RAMP) has assumed a far wider role than its title might suggest. A number of studies have been commissioned and published, including documents on environmental conditions in library and archives buildings, disaster preparedness planning and pest management, some of which have already been cited as the most authoritative accounts in their respective subjects. RAMP led to the development of the Memory of the World Programme which is designed to stimulate new forms of activity to preserve the documentary heritage. Early projects include a CD-ROM containing manuscripts from the National Library of the Czech Republic, and others with manuscripts as diverse as the Radzivill Chronicle from St Petersburg and early Koranic fragments from Sana'a in Yemen (Abid 1995).

Conclusion – but not the end

International conferences, UNESCO reports and European Commission plans can sometimes seem a little remote from the work of the ordinary librarian or archivist, struggling to keep a decaying collection in a condition in which it can be used, often in an inadequate building and almost always with insufficient funds. The perception is understandable, but it is false. A profession, which is by definition self-regulating, creates for itself the climate in which it conducts its activities. Within the broad scope of providing the service demanded by its clients, it largely determines its own agenda. In the last 25 years, and more markedly so in the early 1980s, the library profession in many countries has apparently reached the conclusion, through its various representative bodies, that preservation is an area of significant and serious professional concern. The infrastructure of support offered by national, international and supranational bodies, and the policies they can determine or influence, is the essential foundation upon which action is built. Most libraries in most countries are heavily dependent upon public funding, and public funding is voted by politicians who themselves, in democratic states, have to be sensitive to public opinion. Preservation is not, of course, a major public concern (although conservation in general is an increasingly prominent political issue throughout the industrialized world), but opinion-formers and professional leaders have succeeded in putting it on the official agenda.

By the end of the 1980s, a broad consensus had emerged. There was a general agreement that preservation was important, not least because our central professional activity – to transfer information from source to user – would be frustrated if we were to lose the media that contain the information. Therefore it was argued that we needed to be able to determine whether to preserve information in its original format, or whether to reformat it and preserve the surrogate. To achieve this, technologies were needed that would facilitate this reformatting, and then preserve the surrogates themselves. Techniques were also needed to repair, restore and preserve those damaged originals that could not be sacrificed. In short, ten years of revitalized concern for the physical media of information forced librarians to rethink the way in which we manage our information resources. Preservation, access and use are interdependent, not contradictory.

This approach was not significantly flawed, but it was ultimately inadequate because it was incomplete. What was missing was a full articulation of the need for selectivity in preservation, and a systematization of the way in which that could be achieved. In 1989, the British Library formally and publicly recognized that it could no longer continue to preserve everything as a unique national library of last resort (Enright, Hellinga and Leigh 1989). In itself, this was, to some extent an open acknowledgment of a fact that had driven some aspects of policy for decades, but it was, nevertheless, an important step forward.

In challenging the concept of the universal research library, we have to consider two related issues:

• the **selection** of material and information for preservation
• the provision of **access** to the selected material.

The selection of material for preservation, and the assigning of priorities to it, has already been discussed at some length (see pp. 85–87). Many of the principles that have been suggested, however, can be applied at regional or national level (or indeed by international agreement) as well as by individual institutions. Materials of great historical and cultural importance will still be preserved; but if materials of lesser significance (especially if the future demand for them is thought likely to be low) are preserved only selectively, limited resources can be concentrated on the most important material. In effect, the principle of selective preservation has already been accepted in the archiving of electronic data for reasons of practicality if no other (see pp. 57–67), and it is in fact already applied to some kinds of printed material. Almost all libraries have a disposal policy, and the few which do not (principally the legal deposit libraries) select material before it is accessioned, on the principle that it will then be permanently preserved. Archivists have always understood the principle that selection is a matter of judging which documents will be of long-term significance, acquiring them and disposing of everything else; librarians have taken a different approach by selecting less discriminatingly which is legitimate when it caters for current demands, but then being reluctant to dispose of material when it has outlived its usefulness. It is critical that we begin to look at these issues on a *national* level, so that national policies for disposal and retention can be developed. Nothing will be lost, and much time, effort and money will be saved.

Access is the second key issue, for preservation has no purpose if the material and information cannot be made available to users. We have already discussed some of the specific issues in terms of material of great rarity or value which is properly held in special collections, or access to digital data by networks or on electronic products such as a CD-ROM. More generally, the principle can be invoked that material and information must be accessible, and that it should be preserved in a form which facilitates this. For electronic data, this means regular refreshment; for many manuscripts and archival documents it means repair or other conservation treatment; for some books and most newspapers it means conversion into some other format such as microfilm or a digitized file. The specifics are less important than the general principle: the purpose of preservation is access, and the demands of access will normally drive the choice of preservation strategy.

The future

The first edition of this book concluded with the following paragraph (Feather 1991: 106):

> Preservation is properly seen as one aspect of collection management, the process by which library collections are assembled, augmented and organized for exploitation. It is concerned with all formats and all media. It is concerned with the old and the new. It is concerned with the past. But it is, above all, vitally concerned with the future.

In the five years since those words were written, the changes in the provision of information services in libraries and elsewhere have continued at an ever-increasing rate. Preservation management has not been exempted from that change, and should seek to exploit, not to avoid, its consequences. Powerful new scientific methods have been developed and perfected which give us new tools to combat the old enemies; mass deacidification is the most obvious example, but there are others, such as better quality paper and card, and better techniques for the processing of photographic film – to take but two examples – that continue to be developed. More publishers throughout the world have been persuaded to use chemically inert (so-called 'acid free') paper for their books to help us to avoid repeating the mistakes of the past. Funding bodies and library managers and their governing bodies have shown a greater awareness of preservation issues, and the whole spectrum of those issues (from conservation through format conversion and security to disaster management) has been explored and recognized.

At the same time, wholly new technologies offer both solutions and new challenges. Electronic data will become even more predominant in the future than it has been in the last decade. Many works of permanent value, from reference books to scholarly journals, will be published only in digital form, whether on a CD-ROM (or some digital information carrier still uninvented) or through a network. We already know we can preserve digital data provided we manage the data and the technology properly, but we still have to resolve complex strategic and financial issues about how access is to be managed and funded. Preservation merges almost seamlessly into broader questions about electronic publishing and electronic document delivery. It remains the case that in preserving the legacy of the past and present, we must never take our eyes off the future.

REFERENCES

Abid, A. (1995). Memory of the World – preserving the documentary heritage. *IFLA journal*, **21:3**, 169-74.

Ackerman, M. S. and Fielding, Roy T. (1995). Collection maintenance in the digital library (a paper delivered at the Second Annual Conference on the Theory and Practice of Digital Libraries, 11–13 June). (URL:http://csdl.tamu.edu/DL95/papers/ackerman/ackerman.html)

Allen, S. M. (1995). Using the Internet to report rare book and manuscript thefts. *Rare book and manuscripts librarianship*, **10:1**, 22-37.

American National Standards Institute (1984). *American National Standard for Information Science – permanence of paper for printed library materials*. New York, American National Standards Institute (ANSI Z39.48-1984).

Anderson, H. and McIntyre, J. (1985). *Planning for disaster control in Scottish libraries and record offices*. Edinburgh, National Library of Scotland.

Applebaum, B. (1991). *Guide to environmental protection of collections.* Madison CT, Sound View Press.

Arnoult, J-M., Kremp, V. and Musembi, M. (eds.) (1995). *Proceedings of the pan-African conference on the conservation of library and archival materials*. 2 vols., Munich, Bowker-Saur (IFLA Publications, 43, 44).

Association of Research Libraries (1996). *ARL preservation program.* (URL: http://arl.cni.org/preserv/preserv.html)

Atkinson, R. W. (1986). Selection for preservation: a materialistic approach. *Library resources and technical services,* **30**, 341–53.

Awards (1989) for cataloguing, preservation and purchase. *British Library Research and Development Department research bulletin,* **3**, 5–7.

Banks, R. E. R. (1987). The commercial option: balancing needs and resources. In: Palmer, R. E. (ed.) *Preserving the word. Library Association Conference Proceedings Harrogate 1986).* London, Library Association Publishing, 77–89.

Barden, P. (1994). The British Library image demonstrator project. *Information management and technology,* **27:5**, 214–15.

Barrow, W. J. (1959). *Deterioration of book stock: cases and remedies: two studies on the permanence of book paper.* Richmond VA, Virginia State Library.

Battin, P. (1985). Preservation at the Columbia University Libraries. In: Merrill-Oldham, J. and Smith, M., (eds.) *The library preservation program. Models, priorities, possibilities.* Chicago IL, American Library Association, 34–40.

Battin, P. (1989). Cooperative preservation in the United States. *Alexandria,* **1:2**, 7–16.

Battin, P, (1993). From preservation to access: paradigm for the nineties. *IFLA journal,* **19:4**, 368–73.

Baynes-Cope, D. (1994). Principles and ethics in archival repair and archival conservation. Part 1: the principles of archival repair and of archival conservation. *Journal of the Society of Archivists,* **15:1**, 17–26.

Bell, N. (1994). Considerations when treating paper manuscripts. In: Hadgraft, N., and Swift, K., (eds.) *Conservation and preservation in small libraries.* Cambridge, Parker Library Publications, 101–6.

Beowulf rewarded (1995). *Initiatives for access news,* **3**, 1–2.

Besser, H., and Trant, J. (1995). *Introduction to imaging. Issues in constructing an image database.* Santa Monica CA, Getty Art History Information Program.

Bohem, H. (1978). *Disaster prevention and preparedness.* Berkeley CA, University of California Press.

Briggs, J. R. (1994). Preservation factors in the design of new libraries: a building services engineers's viewpoint. In: Hadgraft, N., and Swift, K., (eds.) *Conservation and preservation in small libraries.* Cambridge, Parker Library Publications, 49–69.

British Library (1993). *For scholarship, research and innovation. Strategic objectives to the years 2000.* London, The British Library.

British Standards Institution (1979). *Processed photographic film for archival records.* 2 parts. London, British Standards Institution (BS 5699 Part 1:1979; BS 5699 Part 2:1979).

British Standards Institution (1989). *Recommendations for the storage and exhibition of archival documents.* London, British Standards Institution (BS 5454:1989).

British Standards Institution (1980). *Specification for 35mm microcopying of newspapers for archival purposes.* London, British Standards Institution (BS 5847:1980)

Broadhurst, R. (1993). *The digitization of library material.* London, Library and Information Technology Centre (Library and Information Briefings, 39).

Buchanan, S. A. (1988). *Disaster planning: preparedness and recovery for libraries and archives.* Paris, UNESCO (PGI-88/WS/6).

Buchanan, S.A., and Jensen, K. (1995). Preservation perspectives. *Wilson Library bulletin,* **69:6,** 53–4.

Burrows, J., and Cooper, D. (1992). *Theft and loss from UK libraries: a national survey.* London, Home Office Police Department (Police Research Group Crime Prevention Unit Series, Paper 37).

Burton, J. O. (1931). Permanence studies of current commercial book papers. *Bureau of Standards journal of research*, **7**, 429–39.

Cains, A. (1994). In-situ treatment of manuscripts and printed books in Trinity College, Dublin. In: Hadgraft, N., and Swift, K., (eds.) *Conservation and preservation in small libraries*. Cambridge, Parker Library Publications, 127–31.

Child, M. S. (1986). Further thoughts on 'Selection for preservation: a materialistic approach'. *Library resources and technical services*, **30**, 354–62.

Clapp, V. W. (1972). The story of permanent/durable book paper. *Restaurator*, **Suppl. 3**, 24–46.

Clarkson, C. (1994). Rediscovering parchment: the nature of the beast. In: Hadgraft, N., and Swift, K., (eds.) *Conservation and preservation in small libraries*. Cambridge, Parker Library Publications, 75–96.

Clements, D. W. G. (1986a). The National Preservation Office in the British Library. *IFLA journal*, **12**, 25–32.

Clements, D. W. G. (1986b). *Preservation and conservation of library documents: a UNESCO/IFLA/ICA enquiry into the current state of the world's patrimony*. Paris, UNESCO (PGI-86/WS/15rev).

Clements, D. W. G. (1987a). Policy planning in the UK: from national to local. In: Palmer, R. E. (ed.) *Preserving the word. Library Association Conference Proceedings Harrogate 1986*). London, Library Association Publishing, 17–26.

Clements, D. W. G. (1987b). *Preservation and conservation of library documents: a UNESCO/IFLA/ICA enquiry into the current state of the world's patrimony*. Paris, UNESCO (PGI-87/WS/15).

Clements, D. W. G. (1988). Preservation microfilming and substitution policy in the British Library. *Microform review*, **17**, 17–22.

Clements, D. W. G., and Arnoult, J-M. (1988). Preservation planning in Europe. *IFLA journal*, **14**, 354–60.

Clements, D.W.G., Butler, C.E., and Millington, C.A. (1988). Paper strengthening at the British Library. In: *Conservation in archives.* Paris, International Council on Archives, 45–50.

Clements, D. W. G., and Dureau, J-M. (1986). *Principles for the preservation and conservation of library materials.* The Hague, IFLA (IFLA Professional Reports, 8).

Cloonan, M.V. (1994). *Global perspectives on preservation education.* Munich, K.G. Saur (IFLA Publications 69).

Columbia University (1996). *Modern social and economic history project.* (URL: http://cul.columbia.edu/cu/libraries/services/preservation/NEH.html [with a link to the Brittle Books Policy statement]).

Commission on Preservation and Access (1991). *Review and Assessment Committee. Final Report.* (Chair: David H. Stam) Washington DC, Commission on Preservation and Access.

Commission on Preservation and Access (1995). *Preserving digital information: draft report of the Task Force on Archiving of Digital Information commissioned by the Commission on Preservation and Access and the Research Libraries Group.* Washington, DC: Convention on Preservation and Access.

Conway, P. (1989). Archival preservation: definitions for improving education and training. *Restaurator,* **10,** 47–60.

Conway, P. (1994). Digitizing preservation. *Library journal,* **19:2,** 42–5.

Cook, M. (1982). *Guidelines for curriculum development in records management and archives: a RAMP study.* Paris, UNESCO (PGI-82/WS/16).

Cunha, G. M. (1988). *Methods to determine the preservation needs in libraries and archives: a RAMP study with guidelines.* Paris, UNESCO (PGI-88/WS/160).

Cunha, G. M., Lowell, H. P., and Schnare, R. E., Jr. (1982). *Conservation survey manual.* New York, New York Library Association.

Dempsey, L., Law, D., and Mowat, I. (1995). *Networking and the future of libraries 2. Managing the intellectual record.* London, Library Association Publishing.

Dewe, M., (ed.) (1987). *Adaptation of buildings to library use. Proceedings of the Seminar held in Budapest June 3–7 1985.* Munich, Saur (IFLA Publications, 39).

Diehl, E. (1946). *Bookbinding: its background and technique.* 2 vols., New York, Rinehart.

Eaton, F.L. (1993). The National Archives and electronic records for preservation. In: Mohlhenrich, J. (ed.). *Preservation of electronic formats and electronic formats for preservation.* Fort Atkinson WI, Highsmith Press, 41–61.

Eden, P., Feather, J., and Matthews, G. (1993). Preservation policies and conservation in British academic libraries in 1993: a survey. *British journal of academic librarianship,* **8:2,** 65–88.

Eden, P., Feather, J., and Matthews, G. (1994). Of special concern? Preservation in perspective. *Public library journal,* **9:2,** 33–8.

Enright, B., Hellinga, L., and Leigh, B. (1989). *Selection for survival: a review of acquisition and retention policies.* London, The British Library.

EPIC News (1996). Announcements: mass deacidification report. (URL:http://www.library.knaw.nl/epic/ecpatex/news.htm# Announcements)

European Commission on Preservation and Access (1996). [Website at] URL: http://www.library.knaw.nl/epic/ecpatex/ home.htm

Fabian, B. (1983). *Buch, Bibliothek und Geisteswissenschaftliche Forschung.* Göttingen, Vandenhoek und Ruprecht.

Farr, G. F., Jr. (1992). NEH's program for the preservation of brittle books. *Advances in preservation and access,* **1,** 49–60.

Feather, J. (1990). *Guidelines on the teaching of preservation to librarians, archivists and documentalists.* The Hague, IFLA (IFLA Professional Reports, 8).

Feather, J. (1991). *Preservation and the management of library collections.* London, Library Association Publishing.

Feather, J. (1995). Training for preservation: needs and provision. (Unpublished paper delivered at the Satellite Meeting of the IFLA Section on Conservation and Preservation, Budapest, Hungary 15–17 August).

Feather, J., and Lusher, A. (1988). *The teaching of conservation in LIS schools in Great Britain.* London, The British Library (Research Paper, 49).

Feather, J., and Lusher, A. (1989). Education for conservation in British library schools: current practices and future prospects. *Journal of librarianship*, **21**, 129–38.

Feather, J., Matthews, G., and Eden, P. (1996). *Preservation management in the 1990s: policies and practices.* Aldershot, Gower.

Feather, J., and Vitiello, G. (1991). The European Register of Microform Masters: a new bibliographical tool. *Journal of librarianship and information science*, **23:4**, 177–81.

Federici, C. (1995). What kind of book conservators in the third millennium? The state-of-the-art in Italy and some proposals for the future. *International preservation news*, **11**, 12–13.

Foot, M. (1994). Aspects of mass conservation. *IFLA journal*, **20:3**, 321–30.

Foot, M. (1995). Preservation policy, dilemma, needs: a British Library perspective. *Conservation administration news*, **58/59**, 1, 3–6; **60**, 5–8; **61**, 6–10.

Forde, H. (1987). Education and archive conservation. In: National Preservation Office. *Conservation in crisis* (National Preservation Office Seminar Papers, 1), 23–7.

Fox, P. (1993). Microforms: still the best hope for preservation? In: National Preservation Office. *Microforms in libraries. the untapped resource?* London, The British Library.

Fredericks, M. (1992). Recent trends in book conservation and library collections care. *Journal of the American Institute for Conservation,* **31:1,** 95–101.

Gartner, J. (1993). Digitising the Bodleian? *Audiovisual librarian,* **19:3,** 22–3.

Getty Conservation Institute (1990). *The conservation assessment: a tool for planning, implementing and fundraising.* Marina del Rey CA, Getty Conservation Institute/National Institute for Conservation.

Graham, P. S. (1995a). The digital research library: tasks and commitments. (A paper delivered at the Second Annual Conference on the Theory and Practice of Digital Libraries, 11–13 June 1995). (URL:http://csdl.tamu.edu/DL95/papers/graham/graham.html)

Graham, P. S. (1995b). Long-term intellectual preservation. In: Elkington, N. E. (ed.) *Digital imaging technology for preservation. Proceedings from an RLG symposium.* Mountain View CA, Research Libraries Group, 41–57.

Gwynn, N. E., (ed.) (1987). *Preservation microfilming: a guide for librarians and archivists.* Chicago, American Library Association.

Haas, W. J. (1972). *Preparation of detailed specifications for a national system for the preservation of library materials. Final Report.* Washington, DC, Association of Research Libraries.

Hadgraft, N. (1994). Storing and boxing the Parker Library manuscripts. In: Hadgraft, N., and Swift, K., (eds.) *Conservation and preservation in small libraries.* Cambridge, Parker Library Publications, 132–40.

Harris, K. E. and Shahani, C. J. (1995). *Mass deacidification reports issues by the Library of Congress.* (URL: http://palimpsest.stanford.edu/byorg/lc/massdeac/)

Harvey, R. (1993). *Preservation in libraries: principles, strategies and practices for librarians.* London, Bowker Saur.

Havermans, J. (1995). *Environmental influences on the deterioration of paper.* The Hague, Barjested, Meeuws and Co.

Heckmann, H. (1987). Storage and handling of audio and magnetic material. In: Smith, M. A. (ed.), *Preservation of library materials* (conference held at the National Library of Austria, Vienna, 7–19 April 1986, sponsored by the Conference of Directors of National Libraries in cooperation with IFLA and UNESCO), 2 vols., Munich, K. G. Saur, vol. 2, 67–73.

Hedstrom, M. (1991). Understanding electronic incunabula: a framework for research on electronic records. *American archivist,* **54:3**, 334–54.

Helal, A. H., and Weiss, J. W. (1996). *Electronic documents and information: from preservation to access.* Essen, Universitätsbibliothek.

Henderson, C. (1987). Curator or Conservator: who decides on what treatment. *Rare book and manuscript librarianship,* **2**, 103–7.

Henderson, K. L., and Henderson, W. T. (1991). *Conserving and preserving materials in non-book formats.* Urbana-Champaign IL, University of Illinois, Graduate School of Library and Information Science.

Hendley, T. (1983). *The archival storage potential of microfilm, magnetic media and optical data discs.* Hatfield, National Reprographic Centre for Documentation (BNB Research Fund Report, 10).

Hendley T. (1996). *The preservation of digital material.* London, British Library Research and Development Department (R&D Report 6242).

Hendriks, K. B. (1984). *The preservation and restoration of photographic materials and libraries.* Paris, UNESCO (PGI-84/WS/1).

Higginbotham, B. B. (1990). *Our past preserved. a history of American library preservation 1876–1910.* Boston MA, G. K. Hall.

Hockey, S. (1994). Electronic texts in the humanities: a coming of age. In: Sutton, B. (ed.), *Literary texts in an electronic age: scholarly implications and library services.* Urbana-Champaign IL, University of Illinois Graduate School of Library and Information Science, 21–34.

Hookham, F. (1994). Preservation factors in the design of new libraries: an architect's viewpoint. In: Hadgraft, N., and Swift, K., (eds.) *Conservation and preservation in small libraries.* Cambridge, Parker Library Publications, 70–3.

Hunter, D. (1947). *Papermaking: the history and technique of an ancient craft.* 2nd ed., New York, Knopf.

IFLA Working Group on Newspapers (1988). The retention or disposal of newspapers after microfilming. In: Gibb, I. (ed.) *Newspaper preservation and access. Symposium held in London, 12–15 August 1987).* 2 vols., Munich, Saur (IFLA Publications, 45, 46), vol. 2, 421–3.

Irvine, R., and Woodward, G. S. (1894). On the presence in paper of residual chemicals used in its preparation. *Journal of the Society of the Chemical Industry,* **13**, 131–3.

Jarrell, T. D., (ed.) (1936). *Deterioration of book and record papers.* Washington DC, Department of Agriculture.

Jensen, M. B. (1993). Copying for the future. Electronic preservation. *Document delivery world,* **9:4/5**, 29–31.

Johnson, R. (1891). Inferior paper. *Library journal,* **16**, 241–2.

Kaltwasser, F. G. (1986). Probleme der Literaturversorung in den Geisteswissenschaften. *ZIBB,* **33**, 92–9.

Kenney, A. R. (1993a). Digital-microform conversion: an interim preservation solution. *Library resources and technical services,* **37:4**, 380–401.

Kenney, A. R. (1993b). The role of digital technology in the preservation of research library materials. In: Mohlhenrich, J. (ed.) *Preservation of electronic formats & electronic formats for preservation.* Fort Atkinson, WI, Highsmith Press, 1–22.

Kenney, A. R. (1994). Erratum. Digital-microform conversion: an interim preservation solution. *Library resources and technical services*, **38:1**, 87–95.

Kenny, A. (1996). Increased deposits on the next century. *The Times Higher*, 8 March 1996, Multimedia Features supplement, vii.

Kiernan, K. (1995). [Material concerning the *Electronic Beowulf* on the British Library Web server]. (URL: http://portico.bl.uk/access/beowulf.electronic-beowulf.html)

King, E. (1986). New hope for decayed paper. *Library conservation news*, **12**, 1–2.

King, E. (1989). New hope for decayed paper: an update. *Library conservation news*, **25**, 2–3.

Kirtley, T. (1992). Setting up a preservation microfilming;ming programme. *Library conservation news*, **36**, 1–2.

Kuberik, M. (1994). EROMM an der SUB Göttingen. *Bibliotheksdienst*, **28:8**, 1207–8.

Legal deposit (1996) of non-print materials. *Research bulletin*, **13**, 3–4.

Library Association (1930). *The durability of paper*. London, The Library Association.

Library of Congress (1980). *A national preservation program. Proceedings of a planning conference*. Washington DC, Library of Congress Preservation Office.

Library of Congress (1982). *Specifications for the microfilming of newspapers in the Library of Congress*. Silver Spring MD, Association for Information and Image Management.

Liddle, D. (1988). Conservation: the public library view. In: National Preservation Office. *Conservation and Collection Management*. London, The British Library (NPO Seminar Papers, 2), 29–38.

Liénardy, A. (1994). Evaluation of seven mass deacidification techniques. *Restaurator,* 15, 1–25.

Liers, J. and Schwerdt, P. (1995). The Battelle mass deacidification process equipment and technology. *Restaurator,* 16, 1–19.

Lievesley, D. (1995). Creating sustainable networked research resources. In: Dempsey, L., Law, D., and Mowat, I., (eds.) *Networking and the future of libraries 2. Managing the intellectual record.* London, Library Association Publishing, 100–9.

Luner, P. (ed.) (1990). *Paper preservation: current issues and recent developments.* Atlanta GA, TAPPI Press.

Lyall, J. (1994). Developing and managing preservation programmes in the south-east Asian and Pacific regions. *IFLA journal,* 20:3, 262–75.

Lyall, J., and Schmidt, J. (1989). *Preserving Australia's documentary heritage: a progress report.* Canberra, Australian Council on Library and Information Services.

Lynch, C. (1994). The integrity of digital information: mechanics and definitional issues. *Journal of the American Society for Information Science,* 45:10, 737–44

Lynn, M. S. (1995). Digital preservation and access: liberals and conservatives. In: Elkington, N. E. (ed.) *Digital imaging technology for preservation. Proceedings from an RLG symposium.* Mountain View CA, Research Libraries Group, 1–10.

McClung, P. A. (1986). Costs associated with preservation microfilming: results of the Research Libraries Group study. *Library resources and technical services,* 30, 363–74.

Maignien, Y. (1995). Digital library: new preservation for a larger scale of access. (Unpublished paper delivered at the Satellite Meeting of the IFLA Section on Conservation and Preservation, Budapest, Hungary 15–17 August).

Mason, P. R. (1995). Imaging system components and standards. In: Elkington, N. E. (ed.) *Digital imaging technology for preservation. Proceedings from an RLG symposium.* Mountain View CA, Research Libraries Group, 25–40.

Matheson, A. (1987). The planning and implementation of Conspectus in Scotland. *Journal of librarianship,* **19,** 141–51.

Matthews, G. (1995). Surveying collections: the importance of condition assessment for preservation management. *Journal of librarianship and information science,* **27:4,** 227–36.

Matthews, G., and Eden, P. (1996). *Disaster management in British libraries: project report with guidelines for library managers.* London, The British Library (Library and Information Research Report, 109).

Meadows, A. J. (1974). *Communication in science.* London, Butterworth.

Merrill-Oldham, J., and Parisi, P. (1990). *Guide to the Library Binding Institute standard for library binding.* Chicago IL, American Library Association.

Middleton, B. C. (1988). *A history of English craft bookbinding technique.* 3rd ed., London, Holland Press.

Ministère de la Culture (1982). *La patrimoine des bibliothèques.* Paris, Ministère de la Culture.

Motylewski, K. (1991). *What an institution can do to survey its own preservation needs.* Andover MA, Northeast Document Conservation Center.

National Preservation Office (1988). *Preservation microforms.* London, The British Library.

National Preservation Office (1989). *The 1988 National Preservation Office competition.* London, The British Library.

National Preservation Office (1990). *Preservation policies: the choices.* London, The British Library (National Preservation Office Seminar Papers, 4).

National Preservation Office (1994). *Preservation: a training pack for library staff.* London, The British Library.

National Preservation Office (1996). *National Library of Australia. National Preservation Office.* (URL: http://www.nla.gov.au/3/npo/npohome.html).

National Preservation Office [forthcoming]. *Piecing together the jigsaw: the framework for a national preservation strategy for libraries and archives.* London, The British Library.

Naylor, B. (1988). Conservation and Conspectus. In: National Preservation Office. *Conservation and collection management. Proceedings of a Seminar 22–23 July 1987.* London, The British Library (NPO, Seminar Papers, 2),19–28.

Neavill, G. B. (1984). Electronic publishing, libraries, and the survival of information. *Library resources and technical services,* 28, 76–89.

O'Connell, M. (1994). Northeast Document Conservation Center at 21. *Wilson Library bulletin,* 69:4, 44–6, 119.

Oddos, J-P. (1991). Politique de préservation et de restauration à la Bibliothèque de France. *Bulletin des bibliothèques de France,* 36:4, 317–23.

Ogden B. W. (1985). Determining conservation options at the University of California at Berkeley. In: Merrill-Oldham, J. and Smith, M. (eds.) *The library preservation program: models, priorities, possibilities.* Chicago IL, American Library Association, 63–8.

Ogden, S. (1979). The impact of the Florence flood on library conservation in the United States of America: a study of the literature published 1956–1976. *Restaurator,* 3:1–2, 1–36.

Parker, T. A. (1988). *Study in integrated pest management for libraries and archives.* Paris, UNESCO (PGI-88/WS/20).

Pascoe, M. W. (1988). *Impact of environmental pollution on the preservation of archives and records.* Paris, UNESCO (PGI-88/WS/18).

Penn, I. A., Pennix, G. B., and Coulson, J. (1994). *Records management handbook.* 2nd ed., Aldershot, Gower.

Petherbridge, G. (1987). Analysis, specification and calculation in the preparation of leaf-casting pulp: a methodology. In: Petherbridge, G., (ed.) *Conservation of library and archive materials and the graphic arts.* London, Butterworth, for the Institute of Paper Conservators and the Society of Archivists, 153–79.

Poole, F. G. (1976). The proposed national preservation program of the Library of Congress. *Library journal,* **101:20,** 2351.

Prescott, A. (1994). Beowulf on the superhighway. *Initiatives for access news,* **1,** 4–5.

Price, R. (1987). Preserving the word: conservation in the Wellcome Institute Library. In: National Preservation Office. *Conservation in crisis.* London, The British Library (NPO Seminar Papers, 1).

Priest, D. J. (1987). Paper and its problems. *Library review,* **36,** 164–73.

Quinsee, A. G., and Macdougall, A. C. (1990). *Security in academic and research libraries.* London, National Preservation Office.

Raphael, T. (1993). The care of leather and skin products: a curatorial guide. *Leather conservation news,* **9,** 1–15.

RBMS Security Committee (1990). ACRL guidelines for the security of rare book, manuscript, and other special collections. *College & research libraries news,* **51,** 240–4.

Ratcliffe, F. W. (1984). *Preservation policies and conservation in British libraries. Report of the Cambridge University Library conservation project.* London, The British Library (Library and Information Research Report, 25).

Reed, R. (1972). *Ancient skins and leathers.* London, Seminar Press.

173

Rees, E. (1988). Wales and the preservation problem. *Library conservation news*, **18**, 1–3.

Root, T.A. (1989). Inhouse binding in academic libraries. *Serials review*, **15:3**, 31–40.

Rüttimann, H. (1994). Saving the memory of humanity: a crisis in the world's libraries. *Logos*, **5:4**, 166–71.

St Laurent, G. (1991). *The care and handling of recorded sound materials*. Washington DC, Commission on Preservation and Access.

Shiel, A., and Broadhurst, R. (1994). *Library material digitization demonstrator project*. London, The British Library (Library and Information Research Report, 94).

Smith, M. A. (ed.) (1987). *Preservation of library materials. Conference held at the National Library of Austria, Vienna, 7–19 April 1986, sponsored by the Conference of Directors of National Libraries in cooperation with IFLA and UNESCO*. Munich, K. G. Saur (IFLA Publications, 40, 41), 2 vols.

Speller, B., Jr (1994). Reconceptualizing preservation. *North Carolina libraries*, **52:1**, 3–5.

Stagg, L. (1995). Locating the microform master. *Select newsletter*, **15**, 8–9.

Stam, D. H. (1983). *National preservation planning in the United Kingdom: an American perspective*. London, The British Library (Research and Development Department Report, 5759).

Stam, D. H. (1991). Organised preservation programs in the United States. *European research libraries cooperation.*, **1:2**, 228–9.

Stilwell, M. (1995). Managing a document's life cycle. *Law librarian*, **26:3**, 416–20.

Swartzburg, S. G. (1995a). Education for preservation: the challenge of access to old and new technologies. (Unpublished paper delivered at the Satellite Meeting of the IFLA Section on Conservation and Preservation, Budapest, Hungary 15–17 August).

Swartzburg, S. G. (1995b). *Preserving library materials: a manual.* 2nd ed., Metuchen NJ, Scarecrow.

Tanselle, G.T. (1988). Reproductions and scholarship. *Studies in bibliography,* **42**, 25–54.

Thomas, D. (1983). Conservation: new techniques and attitudes. *Archives,* **16**, 167–77.

Thomas, D. (1984). Training conservation technicians: an archivist's view. In: Ratcliffe, F. W. *Preservation policies and conservation in British libraries. Report of the Cambridge University Library conservation project.* London, The British Library (Library and Information Research Report, 25), 125–6.

Thomas, D. (1987). *Study on control and security of holdings: a RAMP study and guidelines.* Paris, UNESCO (PGI-86/WS/23).

Tregarthen Jenkin, I. (1987). *Disaster planning and preparedness: an outline disaster control plan.* London, The British Library (British Library Information Guides, 5).

Turner, M. L. (1984). Conservation in the Bodleian: a case study. In: Ratcliffe, F. W. *Preservation policies and conservation in British libraries. Report of the Cambridge University Library conservation project.* London, The British Library (Library and Information Research Report, 25), 127–31.

Van Bogart, J. W. (1995). *Magnetic tape storage and handling: a guide for libraries and archives.* Washington DC, Commission on Preservation and Access.

Varlamoff, M-T. (1995). The PAC Core Programme. (Unpublished paper delivered at the Satellite Meeting of the IFLA Section on Conservation and Preservation, Budapest, Hungary 15–17 August).

Walters Art Gallery (1957). *The history of bookbinding 525–1950.* Baltimore MD, Walters Art Gallery.

Waters, P. (1995). A unique library 'preventive' preservation technology. *International preservation news*, **10**, 8–9.

Weaver, S. L. (1995). Quality control. In: Elkington, N. E. (ed.) *Digital imaging technology for preservation. Proceedings from an RLG symposium.* Mountain View CA, Research Libraries Group, 81–97.

Welsh, W. J. (1986). Experiments with optical disk technology at the Library of Congress. *IATUL proceedings*, **18**, 41–9.

Welsh, W. J. (1987). International cooperation in the preservation of library materials. *Collection management*, **9**, 119–31.

Wilson, A. (1982). For this and future generations: managing the conflict between preservation and access. *Library review*, **31**, 163–72.

Wilson, A. (1988). *Library policy for preservation and conservation in the European Community. Principles, practices and the contribution of the new technology.* Munich, Saur (CEC Publication EUR 11563).

Wittekind, J. (1994). The Battelle mass deacidification process: a new method for deacidifying books and archival materials. *Restaurator*, **15**, 189–207.

Wood-Lee, M. (1988). *Preservation and treatment of mold in library collections with an emphasis on tropical climates.* Paris, UNESCO (PGI-88/WS/9).

Wressell, P., (ed.) (1994). *Current perspectives of newspaper preservation and access. Report of the 2nd national NEWSPLAN conference.* Newcastle upon Tyne, Information North.

INDEX

academic libraries 13–14
access 157
    digital information 67–72
acidic paper 5–6, 7, 38
    see also deacidification
acidity tests 102
adhesives 26
administration 126–37
age, criteria for preservation 86–7
air conditioning 37–8
air quality 47, 99–100
America
    preservation policies 151–2
    research and development
        projects 73–4
    research libraries 4–6
art, computer 62–3
Australia 152–3

Biblioteca Nazionale 3–4
binderies 127–29
binders 132, 136
binding 113–23
biological infestations 45–6, 100,
    115–16
book shoes 112
bookbinding 27–9
bookcloths 25
books
    materials 17–26
    storage of 134
    structures 26–9
Britain 11–16, 144–7
British Library
    conservation problem 11–12

digitization 73
    preservation policies 144–5
buildings
    layout and design 135
    maintenance programmes
        105–6
    preservation surveys 98–100
    security 106–8

case binding 27–8
CD-ROMs 8–9, 56, 57, 68–9
chemical wood paper 21, 22
choice *see* decision making
clients *see* users
codex structure 26
collections
    binding and repair work
        113–20
    preservation surveys 100–3
    preventative measures 111–13
compact discs 33–4
computer art 62–3
computer printouts 30
computer readable data, defined
    76
conservation, defined 2–3
Conservation Branch 11–12
Conspectus 82–4
cooperation 143–4, 150–1
Core Programme in Preservation
    and Conservation (PAC)
    153–4
costs
    digitization 74–5, 131–2
    surrogates 131, 143

craft binding 26–9

damp 41
data *see* digital data
data archives 65–7
data files
 defined 77
 storage and access 68–9
databases
 defined 77
 storage and access 69–70
deacidification 7–8, 9, 117–20
decay 22
decision making 91–5
device specific data, defined 76
digital data
 defined 76
 problems of 9
 selection for preservation 57–67
 storage and access 54–7, 67–72
digital research libraries 58–61
digitization
 defined 76
 facilities 130
 as preservation tool 72–5
disaster control plans 108–11
discs *see* CD ROMS; compact
  discs; floppy disks; optical
  discs; recorded sound

e-mail 62
Eden, Matthews and Feather report
 14
electronic, defined 76
embrittlement tests 102–3
environments, for storage and use
 34–50
European Commission on
 Preservation and Access
 150–1
European Union 150–1

film 31–3, 39, 43
floppy disks 56
Florence, flood 3–4
fold tests 102–3
format
 conversion 119–22

criteria for preservation 86
Foudrinier machines 20–1
France 148–49
fungi 115–16

Germany 149
guarding 29

handwriting, digitizing 54–5
Hollander machines 19
humidity 39–43, 99

IFLA 153–5
information
 see also digital data
 preservation of 8, 51–77
 storage materials 17–50
 use of 84–91
insect infestations 45–6, 115–16
instructions 132–3
Internet 63–5, 71

Japanese tissue 116

keyboarding 54

leaf casting 117
leather 24–5
libraries
 academic 13–14
 American research 4–6
 digital researh 58–61
 national (UK) 12
library binding 28
Library of Congress 4–5, 5–6
light 43–5, 100
Ligue de Bibliotheques Europeenes
 de Recherche (LIBER) 150
linen tape 112

magnetic tape 33, 55–6
maintenance programmes 104–6
materials
 books 17–26
 non-book 29–30
 non-printed 31–4
mechanical wood paper 21, 22
Memory of the World Programme
 154–5

microfilm 8, 119–22
mould 42
mutilation 107–8

national libraries (UK) 12
National Preservation Office
    (NPO) 145–7
newspapers 30, 95, 121–2
non-book materials 29–30
non-printed materials 31–4

optical discs 8–9, 56
    see also CD ROMS; compact
        discs
output media, v. storage media 8–9

PAC see Core Programme in
    Preservation and Conservation
paper 17–23
    see also acidic paper; typing
        paper
    effects of humidity 40–1
    effects of light 43–4
    repairing 115, 116
    temperature changes 38–9
parchment 23–4
perfect binding 28–9
periodicals 29–30
phase boxes 111–12
photographic media 31–3, 39, 43,
    44–5
photographic studios 129–30
pollution 45–7
preservation
    British approach 11–16
    costs 131–2
    defined 2
    history of 3–6
    of information 51–77
    instructions 132–3
    methods 89–91
    new approach to 7–11
    training 13, 137–39
preservation policies
    America 151–2
    Australia 152–3
    Britain 144–7
    development and implement-
        ation 125–40
    European 147–51
    and library use 78–97
preservation surveys
    buildings 98–100
    collections 100–2
    purpose 103–4
    using 104–22
preventative measures 111–13
printed materials 30
pulp 21–2

Ratcliffe report 12–14, 144–5
recorded sound 32–4
Records and Archives Manage-
    ment Programme (RAMP)
    154
refreshment 9
relative humidity (RH) 39–43
repair work 113–23
research libraries
    America 4–6
    digital 58–61
restoration, defined 3
risk assessment 108

scanning 54
security 106–8
selection 57–67, 85–7, 156
selectivity 15–16, 96
shelves 133–4
software, defined 77
special collections 113–14
stab binding 28
staff 134–5
Stam report 145
stock
    financial pressures 10–11
    quality 82–4
storage
    digital information 54–7, 67–72
    environments 34–50
    media 8–9, 17–50
subjects, criteria for preservation
    85–6
surrogates 8–9, 121, 131
surveys
    buildings 98–100

collections 100–2
purpose 103–4
using 104–22

tapes 33, 55–6
temperature 36–9, 99
terminology 76–7
theft 106–7
time factor, preservation policies
   88–9
training 13, 137–39
typing paper 30

Unesco 153–5

United States *see* America
use, criteria for preservation 87
users, effect on library policy
   79–82

vellum 23–4
vinyl discs 33
voice recognition 55

Wilson report 143, 150
workshops 127–29
World Wide Web 63–5, 71